History

of

Cronton

First Published 2004 by Countyvise Limited, 14 Appin Road, Birkenhead, Wirral CH41 9HH.

British Library Cataloguing in Publication Data.
A catalogue record for this book is available from the British Library.

ISBN 1 901231 49 6

*Dedicated to Imelda, Nicholas, David
and all the Grandchildren*

Acknowledgements

I would like to thank firstly, all those who lent or gave me documents, photographs, programmes etc, and to those who shared their knowledge and memories. Secondly to Geoff Lambertsen and his local history gang: Winifred and Joseph Mercer, Ann Atherton, Celia O'Dowd, Don Crowther, Terri Wylie, and later Win Jones. Also thanks to Geoff Lambertsen for typing it up.

And last but not least, to the people of Cronton who kept prodding me on. I hope you got what you deserve! I love you all!

Preface

It is not now as it hath been of yore
Turn whereso'er I may
The things I have seen I now can see no more
William Wordsworth

Cronton was a small village situated between the towns of St Helens, Warrington, Widnes and Liverpool. It has enjoyed a peaceful but rich history, particularly rich in its characters some of whom have found fame beyond the narrow boundaries of the village. Others have been content to do their work and allow that to be their legacy. In the 1960s developers descended and all changed. Within 10 years many green fields, hedges, woods and trees went and Cronton started to lose its identity. The people in the big houses and little cottages alike suddenly found that their homes were very desirable. Even the name of Cronton became desirable as developers on our borders started to use the name to sell their estates. Cronton began to 'acquire' parts of Farnworth, Hough Green, Tarbock, Huyton and Whiston. People buying into these areas wanted to join the village, knowing its worth as we do. Now we are fighting for our life. Cronton is slowly dying as its big brother neighbours edge closer, taking more of our green fields and turning our lanes into mini motorways.

Soon no-one will remember the village of Cronton. We will go the way of other once quiet villages, Moss Bank, Halewood, Halebank, Penketh, Farnworth and Whiston. No trees, no fields, just endless rows of bricks.

This is why I have written down these memories of the village, in order to preserve, at least on paper, what we once had for future generations who may forget where our boundaries lay and what our people were like and how they lived, now lost in the maelstrom of sameness.

Chapter 1

Cronton is a very old village. Stone age axe heads were found in the field at the bottom of Pex Hill (near the reservoir) facing Town End. They were in Liverpool Museum but I understand they are now somewhere in the confines of the University of Liverpool. Cronton was very heavily wooded so perhaps they had only come for the game, but at least they had done some flint knapping so had spent some time here.

It became part of a Norse settlement, presumably under the Danelaw and leadership of Crawenga. The Vikings also had settlements in Cuerdley and in Widnes probably under the same leadership. Documents show variations in the name. In 1242 we were Crohinton. In 1250 Cronton was given to Stanlaw Abbey by Edmund de Lacy with all his land and rights there including the farm of the mill. Other documents name us, Croyton, Crointon, Croenton and by 1562 Crowenston. As we know, spelling was not standardized until the great Dr Johnson produced the first dictionary.

The village formed part of a grant by William the Conqueror for 'services rendered', presumably when he was rewarding friends after 1066. We are in the Domesday Book under Warrington (though not named) in the lands of Roger de Poitiers. Before 1190 part of Cronton was given by Mathew to the Hospitallers, which they in that year granted to William de la More. The Hospitallers were a crusading,

military order founded by the Knights of St John in the late 11th century to care for the sick pilgrims in Jerusalem. The one was called the Higher Schacht (possibly the higher shaw). That part of Cronton was then called Grewinton Halfsnede. The other part was in Whiston. Halfsnede means half of a detached piece of ground. Presumably in Whiston it is Halsnead Park which now fits in nicely with today's Higher Shaw.

Cronton and Whiston shared a leper colony on the Halfsnede. Later Cronton formed part of John of Gaunt's hunting forest along with Cuerdley and other places under the jurisdiction of Halton Castle which was John of Gaunt's hunting lodge. Under the feudal sytem Cronton was a manor in various ownerships.

With the suppression of the monasteries, lands owned by them passed to the King who leased them out. In 1537 the township of Cronton was leased to Thos Tarbock, John Winninton, James Haworth, George Cross and 'others' of Cronton for a rent of £19. 0s. 1d. a year. Later it was sold to Thomas Holt of Gristlehurst. In 1587 it was sold to Thos. Brook by Francis Holt, Ellen his wife, Thos. Holt, his heir and his wife Constance. It was described as the Manor of Cronton, with twenty messuages, two mills and 500 acres of land.

Shortly after it was sold to Thos. Ireland and then in 1598 to James Pemberton of Halsnead in Whiston. In September 1598 James and Katherine Pemberton and their son James sold land to George and Hugh Gresse, Richard Wright, Thomas and John Parr, James Lawton, Thos. Parte, William Norman, Edward Deane and Edward Orme.

Thomas Parte died in 1605. At his death he held his lands by the 'hundreth part of a Knight's fee' (a Knight's fee is explained under the feudal system) John Gleast held land in the same way. He died in 1607 and his daughter, Margaret Lea, aged 55 inherited. Thomas White, Thomas Linacre, John Parr, Francis and John Windle held land in chief by the same fraction of a Knight's fee.

John Parr held two mills in Cronton, a windmill and a horsemill. One mill was for grinding corn the second was a fulling mill. Householders collected their urine which was given to the miller who soaked the woven or knitted woollen cloth in it. Then it was 'paddled' or slapped by the wooden paddles of the mill which was turned by a horse walking around the mill and attached to a wheel. This very effectively felted the cloth thus making it thicker and more proof. It was in great demand for outdoor clothing and shoes.

In 1628 Peter Stock held land in Cronton, his heir was his son William. In 1628 the following paid subsidy for lands; William Parr (son of John Parr born October 1608), William Wright, son of Richard, his heir John died before his father William Orme.

Of interest may be the following: James Lawton, mentioned above died in 1616, his heir was Henry who was two years old. Alas in 1598 James Pemberton sold land to William Norman and allowed him to dig for and stone upon Pex Hill and Cronton Green. Very possibly this was the start of Cronton Quarry. Francis Windle died in 1619, Henry his son was heir. John Windle died in 1621, his son Henry succeeded. To give some idea of the land these men held here is how they were listed at their death:

Richard Cotton died in Cronton in 1604, he held 2 messuages and 14 acres of land

Thos. Parte held 1 messuage, 3 cottages, a toft, 4 gardens, 4 orchards, 10 acres of meadow, 10 acres of pasture, 1 acre of wood, 12 acres of moor and turbary

Francis Windle held 1 messuage, 6 acres of land, meadow and pasture

John Windle held 1 messuage, 1 cottage, 1 garden, 1 orchard, 24 acres of meadow and pasture.

These men did not necessarily live in Cronton, but would certainly have lived in the neighbouring villages.

To understand the feudal system you must know that all land belonged to the King. He granted it to a Knight who gave service to the King in return for the use of the land. The Knight had to provide a number of armed men for soldiering in time of war and must himself serve forty days a year in the event of war. We had several men in Cronton holding land by a Knight's fee who continued to farm their land after the civil war as did others. However, at the restoration of the monarchy in 1660 they did not want to return the land. They insisted the King was dead therefore the land had become theirs. A long legal battle ensued!

The men who owed service to the King had to arm the men whom they sent. Also to ensure that the men had some training Musters were called. In 1553 a Muster was called to see how many men were available in case of war and to make sure they were armed sufficiently and of course be able to use the arms.

Prescot parish provided 67 men and Cronton's contribution was 3.
In the Darby Hundred to which Cronton belonged the Commanders of this Muster were:

> Edward Earl of Derby
> Sir Richard Molyneux
> Sir Thomas Gerard
> Sir Peers Legh
> Sir John Holcroft
> Sir John Atherton
> Sir William Norris
> Thomas Butler of Bewsy
> George Ireland of Hale
> William Tarbock of Tarbock
> Lawrence Ireland of Lydiate

the last four being Esquires.

In return for the serf's service to the Knight for most of the year, (including the work of his wife and children) under the feudal system the serf was granted small strips of land for himself. Each year the

THE

FOLLOWING ACCOUNT

OF THE

MUSTERS OF SOLDIERS

IN THE

County Palatine of Lancaster,

I. MARY, 1553,

Is taken from a curious neatly-written Manuscript, part in Latin; and consists of *De Antiquitate Comit. Lancastriæ*—The *Barons* and the great Holders of Land there about 1814—The Dissolution of the Chantries of Liverpool—A list of all the Chantry Rents there—The King's Rental in Liverpool the 24th year of the reign of Henry VIII.—Divers Charters granted to the town of Liverpool, Richard II. and afterwards—The Book of the Fees, Privileges, etc. of the Dutchy and County Palatine of Lancaster; with many other curious and ancient Documents relating to the Tenants of the Dutchy—The Names of the Purchasers of sundry Chantry Rents in Liverpool. With an account of the Gentry of Lancashire's Armorial Bearings, copied from a MS. written tempo. Henry VIII. comprised in 170 pages, by Thomas Birch, the younger, Armiger, of Birch, tempo. Eliza.—In possession of the EDITOR.

1mo Mary, 1553—In DARBY HUNDRED to raise 430 Men; these were the Commanders of them :—

Edward Earl of Derby, Sir Richard Molyneux, Sir Thomas Gerrard, Sir Peers Legh, Sir John Holcroft, Sir John Atherton Sir William Norris; Thomas Butler of *Bewsey*, George Ireland of *Hale*, William Tarbock of *Tarbock*, Lawrence Ireland of *Lydiate*, Esqrs.

SALFORD HUNDRED—350 Men.

Sir Edmund Trafford, Sir William Ratcliffe, Sir Robert Longley, Sir Thomas Holt, Sir Robert Worsley; Robert Barton, Edward Holland, Ralph Ashton, Esqrs.

LEYLAND HUNDRED—170 Men.

Sir Thomas Hesketh; Edward Standish, John Fleetwood, Roger Bradshaw, John Langtree, Peers Anderton, and John Wrightington, Esqrs.

AMOUNDERNESS HUNDRED—300 Men.

Sir Thomas Hesketh, Sir Richard Houghton; George Brown, John Kitchen, Richard Barton, William Westbie, and William Barton, Esqrs.

BLACKBURNE HUNDRED—400 Men.

Sir Richard Shireburne, Sir Thomas Langton, Sir Thomas Talbot, Sir John Southworth; John Townley, Thomas Catterall, John Osbolston, John Talbot, Esqrs.

LOYNSDALE HUNDRED—350 Men.

The Lord Monteagle, Sir Marmaduke Tunstall; Thomas Carus, George Middleton, Thomas Bradley, Hugh Dicconson, and Oliver Middleton, Esqrs.

And how every Town made them.

HUNDRED OF WEST DERBY.

The *Parish* of Ormschurch 28	Little Crosby . . 4	Sutton . . . 9 —	Bedford . . . 6
Ormschurch . . 3	Litherland . . 3	Parr 4	Aëtley . . . 6
Burscough . . 3	Thornton . . . 4—30	Windle . . . 4	Pennington . . 6
Lathom . . . 7		Rainforth . . . 4	Westleigh . . 6—36
Bickersteth . . 4	The *Parish* of Walton 36	Whiston . . . 3	
Skelmersdale . 4	Walton cum Faza- ⎱ 7	Rainhill . . . 3	The *Parish* of Warrington 25
Scaresbrick . . 7—28	kerley ⎰	Widnes . . . 9 —	Warrington, Orforth ⎱ 7 —
	Liverpool . . . 4 —	Sankey and Penketh 4	cum Sonkye ⎰
The *Parish* of North Meols 9	Formeby . . . 4	Cuerdley . . . 5	Wolston cum Ferne- ⎱ 6
	Kirkdale . . . 2	Cronton . . . 3 —	head ⎰
The *Parish* of Aughton 12	Kirkbie . . . 5	Ditton . . . 3	Burton-wood . 6
	Derby . . . 11	Bold . . . 8—67 —	Rixton & Glassbrooke 6—25
The *Parish* Altear . 9	Bootle and Linacre . 3—36		
		The *Parish* of Winwick 34	The *Parish* of Childwell 27
The *Parish* of Hallsall 28	The *Parish* of Wigan 52	Winwick with Holme 3	Speke . . . 5
Hallsall . . . 7	Wigan . . . 11	Ashton . . . 10	Wolston Parva . 6
Male . . . 4	Ince & Pemberton . 8	Lawton cum Kenyan 5	Garstang . . . 3
Melling & Cunscough 7	Haye . . . 4	Haddock cum Gol- ⎱ 5	Halewood & Halebank 8
Down Holland . 5	Hindley & Abram . 8	bourne ⎰	Allerton . . . 2
Lidiate . . . 5—28	Holland & Dalton . 10	Widnes . . . 3	Wartree . . . 3—27
	Orrel . . . 3	Southworth cum Croft ⎱ 4	
The *Parish* of Sefton 30	Billinge & Winstanly 8—52	and Newton ⎰	The *Parish* of Huyton 16
Sefton . . . 7		Killshaw [Culcheth] 7—34	Huyton cum Roby . 5
Ince Blundell . 6	The *Parish* of Prescot 67		Knowsley . . . 6
Aintree . . . 2	Prescot . . . 2	The *Parish* of Leigh 36	Torbeck . . . 5—16
Much Crosby . 4	Eccleston . . . 4	Leigh . . . 6	
		Tildesley . . . 6	

Everton and Toxteth Park, no return.—EDITOR.

strips were changed so that each had a chance of good land. The serf was allowed pannage which meant he could feed his pigs on the waste or common land. He could also take firewood but only what he could reach by his hook (tool) or his crook in the case of a shepherd, to knock wood off the tree. Hence the phrase, 'by hook or by crook'. He was also allowed to pick up sticks from the ground. Any serf failing in his duty to the knight could be thrown off the Manor. He would not find work on another Manor as Knights 'hung' together and would not take a serf from another. It could also be difficult to marry someone from another Manor because it could only be done with the agreement of the knight. If a serf could not find work elsewhere he was forced to live in the forest as an outlaw preying on travellers.

The manorial system came to an end as a result of the Black Death. Starting in 1346 it raged for several years, killing, according to one estimate, 9 out of 10 people. Labour became so scarce that land was sold off in small parcels to those who could afford to buy. This made the poorer people beggars as their labours were not required for the large estates. Neither of course did they have the security they had on the Manor and they too became outlaws.

The monasteries provided some relief to the poor and the sick until Henry Vlll fell out with the Pope and set about claiming them for himself. Some he destroyed after stealing their gold, silver and books. Others he gave to his favourites which is how a lot of the landed gentry got their houses and land. This meant that the poor could no longer get help from the monks who had either been killed or scattered to join the wandering poor. London's streets became full of people sleeping rough and begging. Thieves abounded and travel became difficult and dangerous because of the outlaws in the forests. Goods could not be transported and disease spread rapidly in towns. Elizabeth 1 acted decisively to settle the problem. She set up the vestries. These were attached to each parish and each had an Overseer of the poor who took money from landowners (tithes) and distributed it in alms to the poor and needy. The Overseer had to be able to write and to count and keep the Account Book. He was assisted by a Constable who saw that there was no breaking of the minor rules and offences such as fighting,

gaming, drunkenness, damage to property, engrossing and selling short weight. These cases were dealt with at Prescot or Farnworth by the Magistrates. Sheep stealing, horse stealing or murder (only murder of men, usually there was less concern about murders of women and children) were dealt with at Preston and it was the Constable's duty to get the Magistrate there. The Hayward looked after the roads, hedges and wandering livestock.

It was obligatory that each householder kept the holes in the road in front of his house in order. They had to be filled in along with any ruts. The wealthier were endangered by poor roads as they were more likely to be travelling on them by horseback. Rutted roads could cause a horse to fall killing or injuring either or both the horse and rider. If a horse had to be destroyed this was the equivalent of a car being written off today and of course there was no insurance.

For cooking people needed cooking pots and the easiest way was to dig up some clay, shape a pot and let it dry. Admittedly not for long but clay was plentiful and you could always make another. But the holes had to be filled up or there would be a fine.

In 1609 the plague was again raging. It was very bad in Cronton and Liverpool according to the book *'History of the Plague in Lancashire'*, by RS France. It is said that the plague was brought to Cronton by a maidservant from Richard Dacre's house in Tarbock. He had a business in Liverpool and the plague infected his family. He should have had his house shut up and his family removed to cabins on the waste (Pex Hill and environs) which were burned after the people had died. He did not want this so he did not report the plague. The maidservant being frightened ran home to Cronton thus infecting the village. Collections were taken in the London churches for Cronton amongst other places in south Lancashire.

The Civil War does not appear to have affected us much. We seem to have been in the middle of it but, rather like the eye of the storm... Prince Rupert crossed the Mersey at Hale and Oliver Cromwell's headquarters for the fighting at Warrington and Preston was said to be

Manor Farm, Rainhill, rather a long way away I would think but I am assured by those who know that a fighting army is always led from the rear. There is a legend that a cave on Pex Hill known as Molly's Top was used as hiding place by a man named Elford who had "supported the wrong side and had to hide from Parliament's revenge". It would seem that at least some Cronton people were Royalists as he was fed until he could safely escape. The cave was where the reservoir now is.

Victories in the Peninsular War were celebrated by raising the flag on the flagstaff on Pex Hill. The flag was attached to an old cross which was destroyed in 1868 when the reservoir was built.

The Overseer spent 2/6d (12½p) when we rejoiced for Lord Wellington in 1813. It was spent on ale.

In the First World War many local men served and as seen by the War Memorial some lost their lives. Mrs G Taylor wrote to each serviceman from Hawthorn Lodge each Christmas. £90 was spent celebrating the end of WWI. Everyone had a good tea in the pavilion (on Pex Hill). There were old English sports and a dance. £6 was left over and was spent entertaining returned soldiers and sailors.

Hawthorne Lodge
X Mas 1917

Dear Boys X Mas is with us again & you are still away from home & those you love fighting in the great war, which looks so dark & long. May we all with 'God' help pray that we may soon be brought to the dawn of a brighter day, when the clash of arms will cease & peace & once reigns on earth. Wishing you all a happy X Mas I remain Yours sincerely Mrs E Taylor

In World War II a searchlight battery was stationed on Pex Hill. Among the men were several Poles. Until the improvements on Pex Hill the gun emplacements could be seen. The guns were to stop the bombers getting to Liverpool, and it worked in a few cases. Some bombs were jettisoned in Cronton and district after which the enemy headed for home. Air raid shelters loomed large in village life after September 1939. Whiston District Council felt that although we may not have been in as much danger as the bigger towns we ought to be protected, and accordingly gave us all one each. Within a few months they were found to be in need of repair (as elsewhere in the country they had been thrown up too quickly). The repairs were done, "as a matter of urgency, the war was not going too much in our favour". The village followed all the instructions of the Government to "Dig for Victory", that is vegetables not trenches! We also collected waste paper and I am sorry to say a lot of Parish Council documents disappeared at this time.

The Wesley chapel was set up as a station for enquiries after relatives and for a feeding centre in case of air attack. It was also used as a centre for the waste paper and clothing. The Roman Catholic School was to be used if the Wesley Chapel was destroyed by the enemy. The schools were used for the distribution of Identity cards, Ration books and gas masks. (I remember several boys being caned for making 'noises' with

their gas masks!). We practised by wearing them in school now and again. Most villagers kept hens and a lively black market swapping eggs for rations went on. The rabbit population declined rapidly too. We had Whist Drives and 'social evenings' to raise funds to send parcels to the serving men. At these events Mr Edward Davies played the mouth organ for the occasional dance. When he really got into his stride he stamped his foot for the rhythm which sent the children into hysterics as the 'big boys' stamped out a counter rhythm. Mr Thomas Darwin, a miner, also sang beautifully at these functions. He sang Richard Tauber songs.

VE Day was celebrated with great jollification. We had tea parties in the schools. You were supposed to go the nearest school but some of the Church members of all persuasions would only go to schools of their own denomination. It was the statues at the Catholic Schools that were mostly objected to. We could not understand it as we hardly noticed them! The homecoming of servicemen and Prisoners of War were celebrated in style with flags flying all over the village and 'Welcome Home' signs in the immediate vicinity of the 'returnees' home. They were given a free tea in the village. We did the same for POW's returning home during the war. These men came home too badly hurt to be combative.

The village settled down again after all the disturbance. The Swedish Government gave the wooden houses in Smithy Close as gift to provide homes for returning servicemen.

The Coronation of Queen Elizabeth 11 was celebrated by the lighting of a bonfire on Pex Hill. Pex Hill was one of a series of beacons which stretched across Britain. The Widnes Scouts lit ours. It was lit by Scout Master Robert Alty when he saw the bonfire on Helsby Hill flare out. The next beacon was said to be Parbold Hill. Unfortunately it was a very wet night and only a few people saw it.

On the occasion of the Silver Jubilee in 1977 the celebrations lasted a week. We had an Ecumenical Service as a thanksgiving. The Parish Council led a procession to Holy Family Church where it was held. The Church was overflowing and numerous people stood outside.

We had a Gala Day which was very very wet. The wearing of 'Wellies' detracted from the country dancing but it has to be said that all the schoolchildren bravely persevered to the end, despite mud flying up in all directions. Each child in the village and any born during the year were given a Silver Jubilee Crown from the parish council. There have been other celebrations of Coronations and Jubilees but I only know of them because of the programmes.

On June 22 1911 events took place on Pex Hill. They were well organised and the different committees wore different rosettes. In the afternoon there were races for schoolchildren starting with girls 3 - 5. Followed an entertainment by scholars of Holy family School. It included a country dance (16th century) by

> P Walton
> Ethel Taylor
> Harriet Atherton
> Nancy Glover
> F Sparkes
> Nellie Glover.

More races for older children followed. Then there was a tea for children and 'old persons' 55 and over. In the evening there were competitions for grown -ups. There was woolwinding for Ladies over 55, a half mile Walking Competition for men between 30 and 49 years. Also a 400 yard Walking Competition for men over 50 years. (I don't think anyone could say they were stretched!) The finale was a concert in the Pavillion by Messrs Firth's and Philips Party.

Part 1. Pianoforte selection by Miss Davies
> A song, "Long Live the King", by Mr Nansen
> A humorous song by Mr D Broome
> Coon Song and Dance by Mr E Firth
> Song by Mr H Firth
> A comic song and dance by Mr C Firth
> Song by Mr F Philips

Part 11 The company presented their Speciality Sketch entitled
> 'Coronation Celebrations in Old Kentucky', by a few of his
> Majesty's subjects. (I don't think news of the loss of the
> American colonies can have reached Cronton). During the

sketch high class solos, duets and trios were introduced as well as up-to-date sand dancing, clog dancing, boot dancing and other musical items. The evening finished with dancing to Pitt and Worell's Band. I wish I had been there.

On May 6th 1935 we had Silver Jubilee celebrations on Mrs Cook's field. The Fancy Dress Parade was led by an Electrical Band. This time nobody over 45 was asked to race. There was an ankle competition for Ladies though! On May 12th 1937 we had Coronation Celebrations. Cups were bought for the children but they were stolen and replacements had to be bought by the parish council. This time there was a fancy dress competition, races and a pillow fight. I remember this. The combatants sat astride a pole with their feet off the ground and hit each other with pillows. The one who fell off first was the loser. I thought it great fun. Later a social evening was held in the Mission Hall and a Whist Drive in Holy Family School. Farrell's the builders gave Whiston RDC a piece of ground by the crossroads in honour of the Coronation which never took place because of the Duke of Windsor's abdication. It was made into a small park and the stocks were moved there for safety because of the increased traffic on the road.

As a footnote to these notes I was recently told of a German TV Dramatisation of 'Fanny Hill, Memoirs of a Lady of Pleasure'. In the opening chapter Fanny describes how she left a small village near Liverpool and went to London. In the notes to the programme the little village was named as Cronton. Fanny got off the coach at the Bell Inn in Wood Street, London where later Richard Wright sent his watch parts.

The War Memorial

Chapter 2

During the time of the Manorial system the poor people belonged to the Manor as serfs to the landowners. All the family, including the children, belonged to the Manor. They were each allowed a strip of land to cultivate, could collect firewood from the forests and could keep a pig that could forage from the forest.

The pigs ate the acorns. This was called pannage, each serf (man of the family) had this right. The firewood could be collected off the floor of the forest and from the lower branches. The wood could not be sawn or topped off but only broken off by a hook (tool) or a shepherd's crook, really just knocking twigs off. From this comes the phrase, 'by hook or by crook', but which we now use slightly differently.

The sick were cared for by the Monasteries, who also fed the old who were thrown off the Manors if they lived long enough to be old and weak. This lasted a long while until various plagues hit the land and destroyed the Manorial system, killing a lot of landowners too.

HenryVIII compounded the problem when he quarelled with the Pope over the legitimacy of his marriage to Ann Boleyn. He tried to abolish the Catholic Church, set himself up as Head of the Church of England and proceeded to claim the monasteries. He either killed or dispersed the Monks giving the abbeys and monasteries as houses to his cronies,

and this is how most of the aristocracy got their lovely homes. Some monasteries he destroyed. The monks had been the saviours of the poor, sick and crippled, providing alms, nursing and shelter for travellers.

By the time of the reign of Elizabeth I, England was in a parlous state. Elizabeth became increasingly concerned about the number of beggars and dying people on the streets, also about the state of the roads. Goods could not be transported safely nor animals driven to market securely. Travellers were murdered and their goods stolen, all this by outlaws living in forests along the roadsides. The Poor Laws were introduced to deal with some of these problems. In each parish what at that time were called 'vestries' were set up. Each parish had to have an overseer of the poor, a Constable and a Hayward. The bigger parishes often also had a Workhouse. These officers were all appointed by the Justices and in Cronton, were sworn in in front of the Stocks.

These men were all appointed to keep order in the parish in various ways. The Overseer had to be someone who could write and 'cost figures' (add up not cheat!). It was his duty to collect tithes from the landowners and to distribute this money to the poor and needy, either as relief or as care. His task was very difficult and was double edged. In the first place he had to make sure that no one got relief unless they really needed it, otherwise the tithe payers could lodge a complaint against him. On the other hand he would be held responsible if anyone in the parish died of starvation. He could be indicted for manslaughter. This Act has never been repealed and is still on the statute book. When I was Clerk to the Parish Council I kept a strict observance of the wealthy people. I was informed of this Act by Whiston Rural District Council when I took office!

The Constable's duty was to see that the market rules were obeyed and that there were no disorderly houses (ie. playing cards or gaming for money), stealing or murder. This only applied to the murder of men, it did not include women or children, they were expendable! Yet you could be hung for stealing a sheep. Theft also meant poaching. Any of the above serious crimes required he put the subject into the Bridewell.

Lancashire, *(To wit.)*

To Charles Woodward and John Critchley

two substantial householders — — — — —
*of the Township of Cronton within — — — — —
in the County aforesaid.*

BY Virtue of a Statute made in the Forty-third Year of Queen ELIZABETH, Intituled, *An Act for the Relief of the Poor:* And another Act made in the Fourteenth Year of the Reign of King CHARLES the Second, &c. We, two of his Majesty's Justices of the Peace and Quorum in and for the said County, do appoint you (whose Names are above-written) Overseers of the Poor within your said Township for one Year. These are in his Majesty's Name to will and require you, that according to the said Statutes you take Order from Time to Time, for this Year to come, for setting to Work the Poor within your said Township; and make a Rate of the Inhabitants of the same, from Time to Time, by a Monthly Assessment, for the raising of a convenient Stock of some Wares and Stuffs in your said Township for the providing of necessary Relief for such as be lame and impotent amongst you: And for placing as Apprentices such Children whose Parents are not able to maintain them, and for the other Purposes mentioned in the said Statutes. And for the better effecting hereof you the said Overseers, together with the Churchwardens, are hereby required to assemble and meet together once every Month, and to take Order in the Premises. And if any in your Township do refuse to pay such Sum and Sums of Money as are rated and assessed unto them from Time to Time for the Use aforesaid according to Law, or any legal Assessment in Arrear or uncollected, than you are, upon a Warrant for that Purpose, to levy the same by Distress and Sale of the Refuser's Goods, rendering the Overplus (if any be) to the Owners thereof; the said Assessments having been first allowed under the Hands of two Justices of the Peace for the said County. Fail not herein at your Perils. G I V E N under our Hands and Seals, this *twentieth* — — — Day of *June* — — in the *sixth* — — Year of the Reign of our Sovereign Lord King GEORGE the Third, over Great Britain, &c. and in the Year of our Lord One Thousand Seven Hundred and *Sixty Seven* —

FIG. I   Appointment of two overseers in Cronton Township.

By Virtue of the Statute Document

Cronton had no Bridewell so they had to be taken to either Farnworth or Prescot. The Constable was also the man who raised the hue and cry after a criminal. This meant that everyone had to look for him in so far as they must not shelter him or withhold information of his whereabouts otherwise they could be taken for the crime too.

The other officer was the Surveyor of the Highways or Hayward. He had to keep an eye out for the state of the roads. He must make sure that everyone did their stint of work on the road. An Act of 1563 said that every householder, cottager and labourer had to work up to six days a year on the roads. Of course as ever the better off people could pay someone else to do their stint for them. Each householder was responsible for the stretch in front of their own house. Potholes had to be filled up. Travel was either by horse or on foot. Imagine if a horse caught its foot in a pothole. The horse could be lamed and put out of action and the rider seriously hurt.

The name pothole comes from the use of clay for making a bowl by the poorer people. Many could not afford crockery and certainly not metal so what did they do? They gathered some clay from the road, moulded it, pressed a hole in the centre, dried it and hey presto! a cooking dish. They didn't last long of course but they could always get more clay, but that left a hole, the place it was taken from...a pothole. It was against the law to leave the hole - it had to be made good again or the Hayward came. He also had to watch for straying animals and take them in the pinfold. Owners paid to get them out. As far as I can make out our pinfold was near the crossroads but how near I do not know. The Surveyor of the Highway worked in conjunction with the Overseer of the Poor. For instance, widows or anyone else applying for relief were put to work picking up stones from the farmers fields. These were put in a sack and carried to the edge of the field, then loaded onto a cart and taken to repair the roads. The Overseer paid the applicants, thus giving the farmers something in return for their tithes, repairing the highways at no cost and giving the applicant relief. A very good system so long as you had a good back! The stones were of course gathered in winter months when the ploughland was resting.

Here are a few items from the Account Book for the repairs to the Highway.

1729   3 loads of paving stones   4/6d   (22½p)

1742   John Knight for 2 tubs of paving stones   1/- (5p)

1734   John Taylor for 9½ days work on the road at 10 pence per day
7/11 (40p)

1742   John Westbrook 1½ days work on the road   1/3 (7p)

1749   Willie Woods   1 days work   1/-   (5p)

The Constables kept their own Account Book, sometimes used to record the paying of villagers for removing pests, for example

1808   paid for birdheads   £1. 14 . 11   (£1.75p)

1810   paid mole catchers   £6 . 5.0   (£6.25p)

1830   Sparrowheads   £1.6.11   (£1.35)

The reason why they were only paid for heads was because they would cook the bodies for food. Moles were counted by tails so that the skins could be used for moleskin jackets. The Constable also had to go for the Coroner and attend inquests. In 1776 he attended an inquest on a child found dead inWidnes where it was decided that it was a Cronton child. His attendance and expenses amounted to 15/7d (76p), a large sum. In 1777 he fetched the Coroner from Widnes when John Lomax's sons were drowned. (I wonder if it was the deep pit in the field behind Town End Cottages. It was filled in when the new estate on Hall Lane was built. Some of the boys had rafts or boats on it and in winter it was wonderful for skating on. I wonder where the water went?)

In 1778 he had to go to Widnes Moor to tell John Webb that he had been balloted for a soldier. This means that names of all men from the constables eligible for soldiers were sent in and then names were drawn out for as many men as were needed. If your name was drawn you had to go to serve. (As usual if you were wealthy you were allowed to pay someone else to serve in your stead). John Webb must have been working at Widnes Moor at a farm. The Constable also had to see that all householders carried out their ash to fill the ruts made by carts in the

road in front of their houses. Mrs Thatcher's idea wasn't original. The Constable also policed the market held three times a week at Town End Cross.

Each householder who made butter would sell the surplus at the Cross on Market day. It is not easy if possible to make a small amount of butter and it could not be kept any length of time so there was always a surplus. Similarly as the water was bad it was better to brew your own ale for drinking and again the surplus could be sold. There was a crime of Engrossing. This means someone buys butter from the maker for say 2p then sells it again at the same market for 3p. Bread that was sold had to be of a certain weight. To sell underweight was a crime, as was putting stone in bread to make it heavier. Another crime was fouling the stream, that is allowing dirty water from middens or sewer pits to drain into the streams (North West Water please note). It was also not allowed to wash meat or fish in streams.

The Constable was responsible for collecting hand tax, window tax and hearth tax. In 1671 the Hearth tax returns for Cronton listed the following

Rich Fithian - 4	John Kent - 1
Gabriel Hoskeyns - 2	Thos. Windle -1
Joshua Turnival -1	John Parr -1
Jane Windle -1	Geo. Greard -1
Eliz. Wright -1	Mary Wright -
John Windle -1	John Prescot - 1
Rob. Darbishire -1	Rich. Winstanley - 1
Will. Glover - 2	Rich Entwistle - 2
Thom. Sefton - 1	Will. Greard -1
Eliz Jamesson - 1	Rich Grear - 1
Will Burkell -1	Rob Burgess -3
Hen. Lathom - 1	
Rob Wilkinson -2	
Savage Rosoor -1	
Rich, Rothwell -1	
Will. March -1	

John Arnold -1
Rob. Wright - 1
John Appleton -1
Eliz. Greard - 1
Thos. Wright -3

He also listed possible jurors, alehouse keepers and helped in taking the Census, which until 1841 just meant a head count.
Appended are some of the Constables who served in Cronton

1776	William Garnett
1777	Henry Rimmer
1781	George Burchill
1793 - 1805	John Hall
1806 - 19	John Parker
1820 - 29	Bryan Warburton
1830 - 31	Robert Parr

The work of the Overseeer was varied. After he had collected the tithes they had to be distributed. He was mainly responsible for the poor and sick but he also had to pay the wages of any man serving in the army. In 1775 he paid James Low three weeks pay at 3/- (15p) and one week at 4/- (20p).

In 1777 William Hindley received five week's pay for £1.2.6d (£1.12½p) He also paid pensions to the elderly. In 1735, Hindley, Swift, and Perry each got 26 weeks pension at 6d (2½p) per week. In 1770 pensioners who were not in the Poor House received £34.11. 6d in total (£34.57p). The Poor House was two cottages on Cronton Road nearest the Catholic Church. The system in the workhouse seems to have been very unfair. Whilst the male inmates had tobacco bought for them out of parish funds, the ladies had spinning wheels bought for them and they had to spin to keep themselves. In 1777 Elizabeth Brown earned 1/11d by her spinning (20p).

In 1778 the workhouse was closed and the inmates were transferred to Widnes workhouse. In 1829 a shandry was hired to take Elizabeth

Plumpton to Widnes at a cost of 3/6d (17½p). Medicine and medical treatment were provided out of parish funds.

Some of the doctors who attended the sick in Cronton were paid for out of parish funds. Zacharias Leaf (Surgeon) of Prescot attended between 1776 -81. William Leaf, an Apothocary, also of Prescot attended from 1776 to 1781. G Parr also a Surgeon and from Widnes, attended in 1787 and J Ollier in 1789. Thomas Windle was lent £1.1.0 to have his child's leg set by Anthony Ranicars.

In1749 Elizabeth Wainwright was bought an 'iron foot'. It must have worked because in a later account she was given 10d for a pair of shoes. Another entry must have had quite a story behind it. It simply states,"expenses paid to to John Rigby's wife when she spent all night trying to get him into Liverpool Infirmary". Jonathan Rigby had been ill and in receipt of alms until 1741. If he suddenly became so seriously ill he would not have stood the journey to Liverpool, at best in a carrriage but more likely in a horse and cart over rough roads. As Liverpool Infirmary was also at that time a mental hospital this could provide an answer. A person could only be admitted to the mental hospital after the most rigorous enquiries e.g. you had to have a pass signed by someone in authority and at this time Sir John Atherton of Cronton served on the board of Managers so he could sign the pass. If he had been suddenly taken violently mental the pass could have been given. He would also have to be free of infectious diseases notably Scabies and be free of fleas. This could have taken up more time. As there were no accounts for funeral expenses or payment for a return journey for him he must have been finally admitted.

Sometimes if a person who lived alone became sick or infirm the Overseer arranged for him or her to be taken into the home of a woman needing relief. She would be paid to look after the person thus killing two birds with one stone.

Children also had schooling bought for them as will be seen in the section on schools. Later on these same children had apprenticeships bought for them.

Medicine Bill

In 1729 Peter Chaddocks's son was apprenticed to the Miller at Tarbock. In 1755 Mary Wainwright's son was apprenticed to a "Captain of a ship at Liverpool". He also had a wardrobe of clothes made for him (made by a local seamstress). In 1762 another of her sons followed the example of his brother. These two boys were presumably not deck hands. In 1762 Wm. Harrisons's lad was apprenticed to a Barber in London. Barbers also did some of the work of doctors at the time. (I won't go into it!)

These apprenticeships didn't always work out though. In 1779 James Low was apprenticed at Liverpool at a cost of £1.8.2d (£1.41p). Either he didn't like it or he had a sense of adventure because he ran away and enlisted for a soldier! He did not like this either so the Overseer paid for his discharge and he came home.

The Overseer paid for material aid too. Coal was collected from the pit and distributed to the poor. In 1741 1/10d was paid for Joshua Rigby to have nine baskets of coal. In 1749 James Rogerson had eight baskets of coal for 4/-. In 1753 Mary Atherton had a load of coal for 1/1d. Clothes were also bought. The following prices may be of interest.

In 1777 Savage Rawson received:
2 shirts value 1/-
1 pair of breeches value 7/6
1 hat value 3/-
1 pair of shoes value 6/-
2 pair of stockings value 3/10d

The shirts were not as good as those received by Mr Edward Worth in 1729. He received three yards of linen at 10d per yard, 6d for thread and making and 2½d for pins. Sometimes animals were bought. In 1735 Anne Rigby had a pig bought for her at a cost of 10/10d. Money or goods were given to help people find work. In 1778 Charles Helsby was given a new spade valued at 4/-. In 1819 Thomas Meade was given clothing and expenses to go to London. This was to the tune of £2.14.4d. Unfortunately he didn't stay long and was given 10/- when he returned. In 1631 was registered a sad tale. 92 years old William

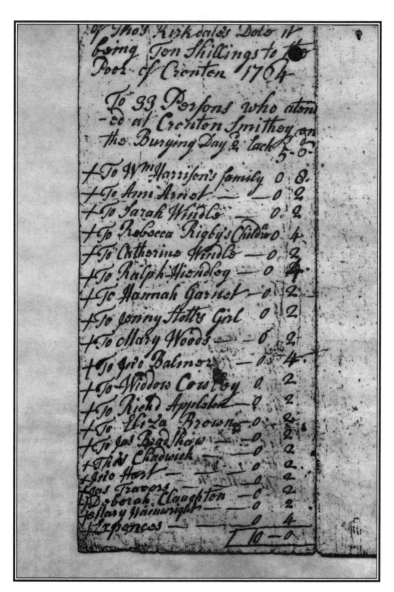

Thos Kirkdale's Burial Dole

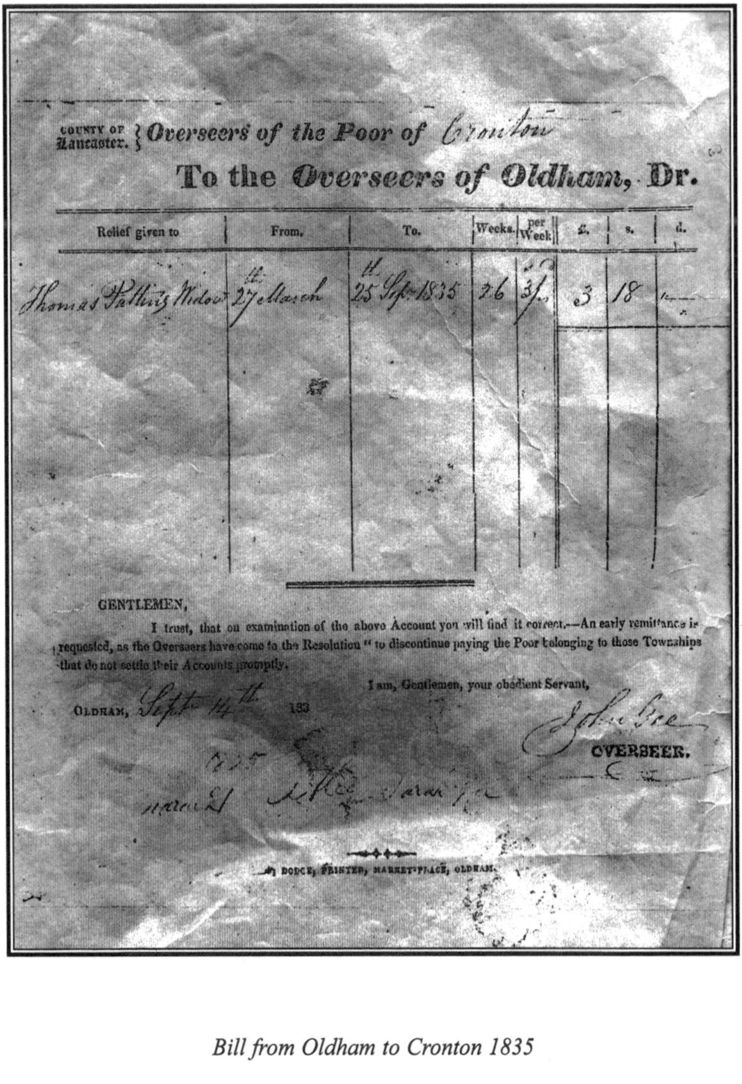

COUNTY OF Lancaster. } *Overseers of the Poor of* Cronton

To the Overseers of Oldham, Dr.

Relief given to	From.	To.	Weeks.	per Week	£.	s.	d.
Thomas Pattin's Widow	27th March	25th Sept 1835	26	3/-	3	18	—

GENTLEMEN,

I trust, that on examination of the above Account you will find it correct.—An early remittance is requested, as the Overseers have come to the Resolution " to discontinue paying the Poor belonging to those Townships that do not settle their Accounts promptly.

I am, Gentlemen, your obedient Servant,

OLDHAM, Sept 14th 183

John Bee

OVERSEER.

DODGE, PRINTER, MARKET-PLACE, OLDHAM.

Bill from Oldham to Cronton 1835

Glover of Cronton who had laboured all his life at his calling of husbandman "requested and obtained relief" because he was unable to work "by reason of his old age or otherwise by the judgement of God".

The Overseer also had to provide relief for people passing through Cronton. Vagrants were given money and 'shown' over the border in case they became ill or died in the parish thus necessitating more expense.

In 1762 two sick ladies were given 2/- and helped over the border. (I can understand this perfectly. When I was Parish Clerk an armchair was dumped in Sandy Lane. I needed to know which side of the border it was on so that I knew whether to ring Whiston or Widnes to have it removed. Argument raged and one Councillor said he would go to see it. He came back and I asked, "So is it Widnes?" The answer, "It is now!". Just a little aside to show you that history is more of the same!).

In 1742 two disbanded soldiers were given 1/- to pass through. This was the only way an ex-serviceman could have got home. They didn't get travel passes. They walked through the parishes receiving relief along the way. In 1819 two strange sailors were given 2/6d! The Overseer also had to deal with legal matters concerned with the villages.

For example, in 1727 Mary Whittle and her son moved from Little Woolton into Cronton and became very quickly chargeable to the parish. The Overseer applied to the Overseer of Little Woolton for support from their rates. Little Woolton refused and the matter came to court where a Removal Order was granted to remove Mary Whittle and her son.

It worked the other way too. In 1835 Cronton paid the Overseer of Oldham £3.18.0d in respect of a widow of a Cronton man. In 1774 James Hunter deserted his wife. The Overseer borrowed a horse and pursued him to Poulton-le-Flyde. James didn't want to return but the enterprising Overseer bought his dinner and talked to him until he agreed to return. This cost the ratepayers 15/- in all. In 1778 it cost a

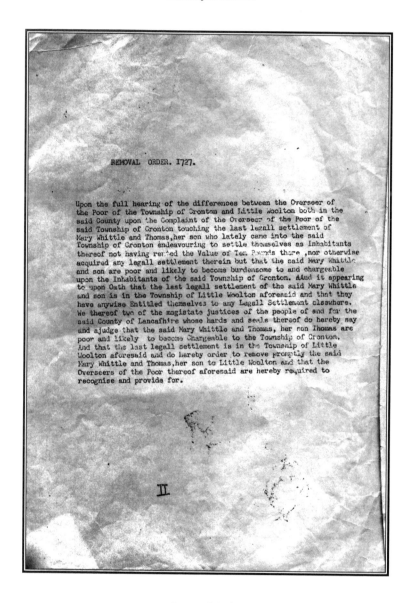

REMOVAL ORDER. 1727.

Upon the full hearing of the differences between the Overseer of
the Poor of the Township of Cronton and Little Woolton both in the
said County upon the Complaint of the Overseer of the Poor of the
said Township of Cronton touching the last legall settlement of
Mary Whittle and Thomas,her son who lately came into the said
Township of Cronton endeavouring to settle themselves as Inhabitants
thereof not having rented the Value of Ten Pounds there ,nor otherwise
acquired any legall settlement therein but that the said Mary Whittle
and son are poor and likely to become burdensome to and chargeable
upon the Inhabitants of the said Township of Cronton. AAnd it appearing
to upon Oath that the last legall settlement of the said Mary Whittle
and son is in the Township of Little Woolton aforesaid and that they
have anywise Entitled themselves to any Legall Settlement elsewhere.
We thereof two of the magistate justices of the people of and for the
said County of Lancafhire whose hards and seals thereof do hereby say
and ajudge that the said Mary Whittle and Thomas, her son Thomas are
poor and likely to become Chargeable to the Township of Cronton.
And that the last legall settlement is in the Township of Little
Woolton aforesaid and do hereby order to remove promptly the said
Mary Whittle and Thomas,her son to Little Woolton and that the
Overseers of the Poor thereof aforesaid are hereby required to
recognise and provide for.

II

Removal Order

great deal of money to take Samuel Cookson, a blacksmith, to Preston, who was charged with abuse. Usually this would be dealt with at Farnworth or Prescot so it must have been for something serious. A receipt was given for his body so he must have been kept there.

A copy of an account book of Mr Harry Wright for the year 1726 shows that the Overseer was out of pocket by 6/7d.

Of course people died and funerals had to be paid for. We owed Farnworth parish 9/9d (50p) when Martha Bradshaw was buried in 1870. Earlier in 1729 Hannah Tyrer and Margaret Harrison were buried at Farnworth it cost 3/4d each (16p). In 1756 the coffin for Jane Arnett cost 6/- (30p). The expenses at Farnworth were 1/4d (6p) and the company at the house drank two gallons of ale before the corpse was taken out. This cost 2/4d (12p). The coffins were made by the village joiner. One was named James Travers.

When a rich person died he would leave money to be distributed to any villagers who stood at the side of the road when his coffin went by. In 1764 Thomas Kirkdale left money to thirty three persons who stood at Cronton Smithy on the burial day. They all signed with a cross. The Catholics signed + but it was generally x and when a document was signed with an x it was customary to kiss as a sort of seal. Hence sealing letters with a kiss is still used today as a declaration of honesty. Also each year several doles were divided. One was Thomas Windle's Dole, a yearly charge of £2.10.0d on the Townsend House given to the people of Cronton. Another was William Glover's gift of £1 a year charged on Lands at Whiston. Another was in Mr Richard Wright's hands called Aughton's Dole.

They were all distributed on the 2nd of July, I would love to know why on that date. The greatest trouble for the Overseer was if a girl became pregnant when unmarried. If the man didn't want to marry her or she did not want to marry him this could become a great drain on the parish resources. A husband must be found and it was the Overseer's job to do this. I have read several village books and diaries where this happened and no doubt it happened in Cronton too. The Overseer would question

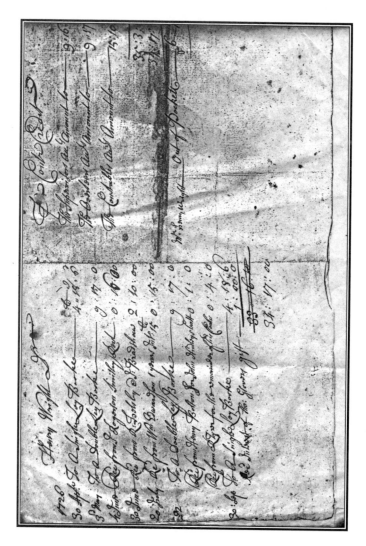

Harry Wright's Account Book

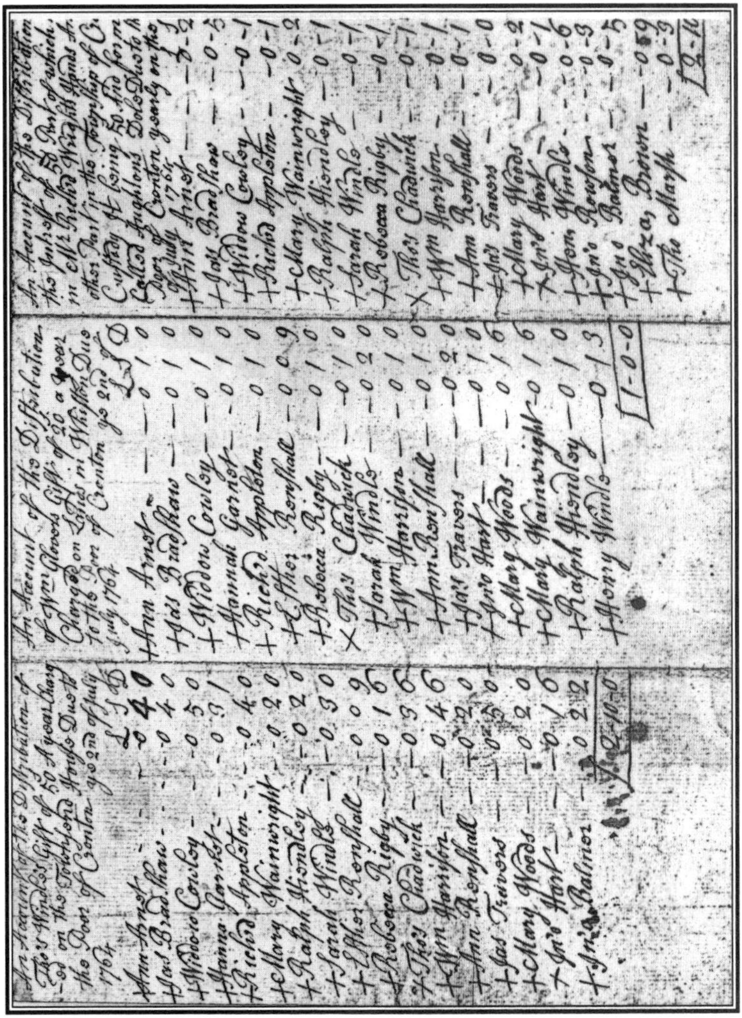
An Account of the Distribution of Tho's Windle's Gift of 50 A year Charg-ed on the Townsend House Due to the Poor of Cronton ye 2nd of July 1764

	£	S	D
Ann Arnot	0	4	0
Jas Bradshaw	0	4	0
Widdow Cowley	0	5	0
Hanna Garnot	0	3	1
Richd Appleton	0	4	0
Mary Wainwright	0	2	0
Ralph Hiondley	0	2	0
Sarah Windle	0	3	0
Esther Ronshall	0	0	9
Rebecca Rigby	0	1	6
Tho's Chadwick	0	3	6
Wm Harrison	0	4	6
Ann Ronshall	0	2	0
Jas Travers	0	5	0
Mary Woods	0	2	0
Jn'o Hart	0	1	6
Jn'o Balmer	0	2	2
	2	10	0

An Account of the Distribution of Wm Gloover's Gift of 20 a year Charged on Lands in Whiston Due to the Poor of Cronton ye 2nd of July 1764

	£	S	D
Ann Arnot	0	1	0
Ja's Bradshaw	0	1	0
Widdow Cowley	0	1	0
Hannah Garnot	0	1	0
Rich'd Appleton	0	1	0
Esther Ronshall	0	0	9
Rebecca Rigby	0	1	0
Tho's Chadwick	0	1	0
Sarah Windle	0	2	0
Wm Harrison	0	1	0
Ann Ronshall	0	1	0
Ja's Travers	0	2	0
Jn'o Hart	0	1	0
Mary Woods	0	1	6
Mary Wainwright	0	1	6
Ralph Hiondley	0	1	0
Henry Windle	0	1	3
	1	0	0

An Account of the Distribution the Intrest of 50 Part of which in Mr Richd Wright's Hands A[...] other Part in the Township of C[...] Custody It being 50 And form[...] Called Aughtons Dole Due to [...] Poor of Cronton yearly on the [...] of July 1764

	£	S
Ann Arnot	0	2
Jas Bradshaw	0	5
Widdow Cowley	0	1
Richd Appleton	0	1
Mary Wainwright	0	2
Ralph Hiondley	0	1
Sarah Windle	0	1
Rebecca Rigby	0	1
Tho's Chadwick	0	1
Wm Harrison	0	1
Ann Ronshall	0	1
Ja's Travers	0	0
Mary Woods	0	2
Jn'o Hart	0	1
Hen. Windle	0	6
Jn'o Rowson	0	3
Jno Balmer	0	5
Eliza Brown	0	5 9
Tho Marsh	0	3
	2	1[...]

the lady. No one in their right mind in those days (or now) would marry the ploughboy if they could get the farmer, or even better the Squire's son. The Overseer would only really get to know about the pregnancy when it beame really obvious which gave him about three months. He would visit the lady who would give him a 'name'. He would then visit the 'name' who would of course deny it. He might suggest another. A further visit would follow. Often if the girl did not fancy being married to the father she would give any name hoping to keep the fun going until the child was born when the parish had to accept it. Great fun and scandal ensued. In the 'Diary of Thomas Turner', when he was Overseer the girl actually named him to his great consternation. (He fell off his horse!). The local Priest or Minister could be named. Men walked around in dread. The shoe could be on the other foot if the girl was anything like a beauty. Someone might own up knowing that she wouldn't look at him in the ordinary way and call her bluff. The Overseer would grab at this and she would be led to the altar - sometimes in the nick of time, sometimes actually in labour. I wonder if this sort of thing caused 'Peg Pusey' to committ suicide.

Chapter 3:

The Village

The name appears in the Testa de Nevill as Grohinton. From the first Census in 1801 the population has been as follows:

1801	311		1861	412
1811	334		1871	427
1831	358		1881	457
1841	402		1901	538
1851	440			

Cronton Hall

Town End is the oldest part of Cronton and is now a conservation area with several listed sites. Cronton Hall was rebuilt in the mid 18th Century after a fire, thus the ground floor is much older than the rest of the house, and some parts of this are older than others.

Cronton Hall 1910s

It has a secret passage which runs under the track to Rainhill and was used during the religious persecution of Catholics. It runs from the Hall to Manor Farm. Several priests said Mass secretly in this area, and no doubt came to Cronton too. The Wright family lived at the Hall for several generations. The Blundell family of Crosby Hall came for hare coursing and dinner regularly, and the invitation was reciprocated as is revealed by the Blundell Diaries.

Later occupants were the Longton family and on July 20th 1880 a dance was held to celebrate a wedding. A dance card which survives lists the Polka, Waltz, Lancers, Galop, Quadrille and Schottische. The Stapleton-Bretherton family bought the Hall with the rest of the Cronton Estate in 1821 and the farms were held by tenant farmers until recently. There is a map in existence from 1819 showing the land belonging to Cronton Hall. The names of fields are given and are very evocative, Daisy Field, Vetch Field, Horse Pasture, Barn Field, Foot

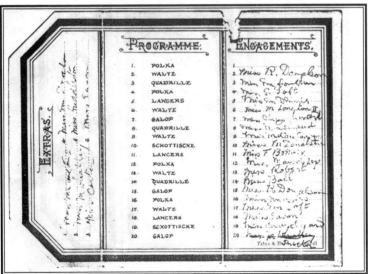

Longton Family Wedding Dance Card

Road Field, Slat Hey, Leach Hey, Alder Hey, White Hey, Mount Pleasant, Hill Croft, Nearer Hay Hook, Farther Hey Hook, Fog's Meadow and   Old Meadow.

Town End Farm was built in 1705 (probably rebuilt onto an older foundation). An old mounting block for getting on horses is found near the front gate. Stone Cross Farm was built in the 17th century again probably upon older remains. It has bricked up windows probably to avoid paying Window Tax on glazed windows (1695-1851).

Town End Cottages

Town End Cottages are built of hand made bricks of local clay. They were originally a barn until the early 1800s. Willow window frames are still in place in one of the cottages and some wattle and daub walls. Roof beams are tree trunks, and the main beam which runs through all three cottages is one tree trunk, the ADZE marks can still be clearly seen. The plaque read 1717 WTA which stood for Windle, Thomas and Anne (but was incorrectly painted later). The buildings were built upon the foundations of 16th Century cottages.

Sunnyside Cottage is a cruck cottage, sandstone foundations for part and handmade bricks as above. Some parts were added later. One end was formerly a barn. There was a priest's hiding place under the stairs. All the foregoing houses form the Cronton Conservation Area.

Georges Hall is an old building but has been changed into two cottages. Welchman's Farm must be mentioned even though it has been demolished. It was built in 1660 and Henry Travisse who lived left a will in which was the following condition: "Anyone owning the house must give £10 a year to Leigh Parish Church". On Maundy Thursday this was given to forty people who attended the service. Henry Travise is buried in Leigh Church Yard. I was told that although the original house was demolished the new house must continue to bear the dole.

Rock Cottage

Opposite the old Unicorn Inn is St Anne's Well. This was famous in the 18th century for curing rheumatic fevers. People travelled to Cronton to drink the water and some stayed at the Unicorn. It was sealed in the early 1900s when a sheep fell in it. It was a spring which spurted constantly and the water flowed away into the Holy Brook, now also drained away. Along with churches dedicated to St Anne it may owe its

name to the mother of Mary, mother of God. When religion was led by the Druids they worshipped springs and fire. San Tan meant Holy Fire and was important in Druidic rites.

When Christianity came to Britain the people were persuaded to adopt the new religion but still hankered back to their old gods. As a compromise they built churches on or near the old holy sites and called them St Ann (near enough San Tan) and thus hedged their bets. Our well or spring could perhaps have been a holy place in the past, and that may have given it its repute as a healing spring.

Close to the well stands the present chip shop. It is a four square building and looks like toll houses from other parts of the country. I wonder if it is our toll house. After all the A5080 was a toll road and I can see no reason why Cronton would not charge travellers for using the road given that the village was responsible for the maintenance of it.

The Stocks

Stocks were first installed for punishment in 1350 and possibly ours date from then. The Cronton Stocks are unusual in that they have five holes instead of the more usual two or four. Only two or three stocks

in the country have five holes. They were still in use in 1799 because in that year the Overseer bought a new stool for the stocks. They were moved to their present site, Coronation Gardens, by Whiston R.D.C. in 1955. The land for the gardens was donatd by Farrell's the builders in 1935 and a garden was made to celebrate the Coronation which never took place. It was deemed a safer place for the stocks than their previous position opposite the Unicorn and behind St Ann's Well because of more traffic using the road. They were repaired some years ago after damage caused by villagers putting bridegrooms in them on the night before their weddings. They had to be released by firemen.

The Smithy was a very old building and was very important to travellers and farmers (and mothers with broken prams). Apart from shoeing horses, mending ploughs, harrows and other farm equipment, the Smith, if he wasn't too busy would repair household ironware. In the time of the drovers when cattle and geese were ferried from Liverpool and then driven to various places inland, Cronton Smithy was important as one of a line of smithies where cattle and geese were shod. The cattle had half clips put on their feet and the geese had their feet tarred and were then driven through fine grit or sand thus strengthening their feet. If this wasn't done cattle and geese walking the rough roads would soon have damaged feet and would either have died or been killed.   The Smith's name for several years was Samuel Cookson who lived at School House. One of the Samuel Cooksons had to be taken to the Assizes at Preston in 1778. The records say, "for abuse" but it must have been something more serious as the Overseer was given a receipt "for his body" and he was kept there. The Constable ordered two men to help him get Samuel there as he was a big man. They were paid one shilling each and meals were bought for them on the way. The Smith paid rent to the Overseer for the Smithy. In 1993 the Smithy was demolished to make an extension to the chip shop.

Opposite the Smithy in Smithy Lane stands a pebble dashed house. This too is old and was once known as the old Beehive Inn. On the sign was the following verse:

Within this hive, we're all alive
Good liquor makes us funny
As you pass by step in and try
The flavour of our honey

I understand several old inns in the country had the same verse on their sign. I do not know who the poet was. It became a chip shop. It later became a newsagents and later still part was an antique shop. It is now a private dwelling house.

The School House was sometimes known as 'Oculshaw' after the owner Richard Oculshaw, and was also known as Grice's House. This house has had an eventful history. Deeds appertaining to this are in the ownership of Cronton Parochial Trust. Most are leases. The Bond of Indemnity in 1765 is an interesting document. The monies from the land were to pay for the birth, maintenance, education and bringing up of the son (James Low) of Ann Henshaw, a single woman of Cronton, so that they were not charged upon the Parish of Cronton. They were fortunate people! I would very much like to know the story behind it all. In the documents it is noticeable that the men could all sign their names. The woman signed with an x (+ if you were Catholic). Perhaps the names and occupants of the people in the documents would be of interest:

Richard Oculshaw, was a yeoman of Standish
Alice Akidd, a widow of Widnes
Lydia Akidd her daughter, later dwelt in Prescot
Richard Gee, watchmaker of Cronton
Robert Johnson, chapman of Farnworth
Samuel Cookson, Blacksmith of Cronton
Thomas Alleby, Husbandman of Cronton
John Atherton, Esquire of Prescot
Thomas Lyon, Esquire of Warrington
Joseph Hamlet, Yeoman of Cuerdley
Peter Harrison, Yeoman of Penketh
John Culcheth and Richard Prior (Overseer to the Poor in Cronton in 1765)

School House

Later it became School House obviously when it became the school.

Several of the older Crontonians received their education there. One of the scholars a little girl, received severe burns to her face whilst attending during the early years of the century. Her pinafore caught fire and as she threw up her hands they unfortunately caught in her pinafore and took the flames to her face. She carried the scars for life. According

Bear's Paw Cottages (The Old Work House)

to the census returns in 1841 John Postlethwaite was the schoolmaster and in 1851 he was still master and his wife was the schoolmistress. Ellen Alcock who lived at Bear's Paw was also a schoolmistress. In 1861 William Morris was Schoolmaster and in 1871 it was Hannah Glover.

Bear's Paw Cottages

Later still the Parish Council met there. During the Second World War it was the Air Raid Warden's post. Now it is a private dwelling house. Bear's Paw Cottages: The house is now two dwelling houses (with several gables) and was once the Cronton Workhouse. When it closed Esther Plumpton was taken to Widnes Workhouse in a shandy paid for by the overseer. The old men in the Workhouse were bought pipes and tobacco. The old ladies were bought a spinning wheel and they had to spin to earn ther living (there was of course no Equal Opportunities Commisssion, just an Overseer). Farther along the road toward Widnes standing well back from the road is another house, once two houses now one. This was the first Dame School in the area. The children had to take a penny each for coals for the fire. Margaret Wright who lived at Cronton Hall left £10 in her will to buy books for the school.

Town End Cottages

Sunnyside Farm, Town End

Stonecross Farm, Town End

Town End Farm

The Unicorn Inn

Methodist Chapel

Cronton Hall

St. Anne's Well

C of E Mission

Bear's Paw Cottage (The Workhouse)

The Beehive Pub

School House

The Black Horse

The Stocks

Holy Family Church

The Cross

Field House: At the side of this house was an old house, until recently the remains could be seen. This is where Charles Leadbetter was born in 1851. His father made sundials there.

Sunnyside Farm (Chapel House): This house too is old but like others has been rebuilt on older foundations. This happened many years ago, owners would not desert a semi derelict building and rebuild again somewhere else. Land was too precious for food and stock so buildings were built on old foundations On the old house at one time was a plaque on the side facing the road. It was an insurance sign bearing a big sun. This was in case of fire, firemen would only put out a fire if the house was insured or the owner produced money up front. If you didn't show a sign and had no money you had to rely on yourself and neighbours.

Sunnyside Farm

Pex Hill was the common ground for Cronton where pigs could panage (e.g grub for acorns) and where the serf could get sticks. Pex Hill was also used during plague years. Cabins were built in which to put plague victims until they died, when they were burnt along with the wooden

cabins. It is also one of a string of beacons which run across the country (it was much higher until the reservoir was built). These gave warning of danger by the lighting of bonfires at the highest point. We received or signalled Helsby Hill and passed on or received a message from Parbold Hill. This way alarms were spread across the country.

There is a legend about a girl who lived at Cronton Hall. She was named Peg Pusey, a maid servant. She was courted by the son of Sir John Atherton of Bold Hall. (There were several Sir Johns so I do not know which one). She became pregnant and of course Sir John's son couldn't marry a servant girl, so Peg threw herself off Pex Hill and killed herself.

The deep footpath leading from Hall Lane to Pex Hill, known as Mill

The Cross

Lane, along with the deep footpath through the fields passing Cronton Hall to Rainhill, are very like the Anglo Saxon Hollow ways. These were land divisions and stopped animals straying. This is only my own observation and belief and I am no authority but I would like to see them preserved.

The Cross at Town End is very old and was a market Cross where excess food could be sold, bread, butter, ale, eggs and cheese. It was also where proclamations could be made such as announcing the death of the King. It had a square stone which

went around the top 'finger'. This has been displaced and was leaned up against the side of Hall Lane. It disappeared to make a rockery when the new houses went up in Hall Lane in the sixties - sad! The markets were held two or three times a week and were strictly regulated. You could not buy butter or eggs from someone and then sell them on at a higher price. This was called engrossing (it is what happens to sheep as they travel around Britain and the rest of the world now. It is the same system now legalised). Years ago you could be taken to the parochial court in Prescot or Farnworth. As everyone knows you cannot make a small amount of butter or cheese, so you made a lot and sold the excess because without refrigerators it would go rancid quickly. Loaves had to be of a certain weight. Sometimes dishonest housewives would add grit or sand to the flour or even put a stone in the middle of the dough to get the correct weight. This was also a court offence. The Prescot Court records are full of people fined for these offences.

In 1621 Ann Webster was fined 3s.4d for engrossing which was a lot of money. She was a slow learner, for she was fined 3s 4d in 1624 and again in 1625! In 1624 twelve persons were fined for making and selling bread under weight, some of them from Cronton. Because water was unfit for drinking, excess ale was also sold by the simple method of putting a branch outside your window or door as a sign of trading. It is not easy to make a small amount of ale so large amounts were made by housewives in turn. It sort of sterilized the water, at least that was the theory.

Higher Shaw Farm is no longer in Cronton but was at one time. A hedge at this farm dates back several hundred years (discovered when there was a dispute about a footpath recently). A house known as Hospitaller's Schacht or Shaws in Cronton was mentioned in the grant of lands by Richard de la More to provide money for the Crusades and it could be that this farm was the one to provide that money.

Holly Farm was a lovely old house where the Glover family (watchpart makers and farmers) lived. One of the sons, Peter, did not want to watch make or farm so he ran a small shop there. It was destroyed by a builder in the 1960s to make way for a new house. He had to rebuild it as near as possible.

Stocks Cottage is another old house next to the Unicorn, also at one time inhabited by watch part and toolmakers. Wayside on Pex Hill is another of our old houses.

Chapter 4:

The Religion of the Village

The Wesleyan Chapel in Chapel Lane was built in 1845 and it and its members over the years have given life and form to the village.

It started in 1818 when James Glover of Sutton met Mary Preston of Prescot when they attended service at Prescot chapel. (He was in love with both Mary and her sister and could not make up his mind which to marry. It was decided one very wet Sunday evening when James had neither overcoat nor umbrella. Mary's sister remarking that it was a poor night put up her umbrella and strode away. Mary only had a cape but offered to share it with James and the decision was made!). They married shortly afterwards and came to live in Cronton on a smallholding, Rose Farm in Chapel Lane.

On settling in Cronton Mary was horrified to learn that there was not one place of worship in the village. Each Sunday James and Mary travelled in the covered waggon to Prescot for the morning service. In the evening she started a service in her own kitchen. Mary and James had seven sons and the worshippers in the kitchen increased. Later they moved to Holly Farm where James and his sons carried on the trade of watchpart making in a watchmaker's shop adjoining the house. The shop was reached by stairs and underneath a greengrocer's shop was opened by one of the sons, Peter who did not take to watchmaking. They also employed several apprentices. Mary cared for her family and

the apprentices also helped on the farm at harvesting. Mary had her relaxation, she smoked a clay pipe and had a snuff box. She deserved it!

One of the sons, John married Mary Ann Cave, also of Prescot and she followed her mother-in-law's example and had services at her own home. Eventually the numbers were too great and the bold decision was taken to build a chapel. Everyone did his share of the labour. James carted all the stone from Pex Hill Quarry. It cost £242 to build and was opened in November 1845 by the Rev WL Thornton. The early services were marred by the fact that when the members were going in the chapel they were ridiculed by the Catholic boys who also threw stones at the windows whilst the service progressed. (The Catholic boys should, no doubt, have been attending their own Church which was in Prescot so they should not have had the energy to stand and throw stones or insults!) Nevertheless, for the time being shutters had to be erected to save them from stones. In 1876 the Sunday School was built for the children.

"A group of old time members" at the Pageant. Back row: Thomas Odgers, James Hewson, Walter Glover, William Cornes. Front row: Mesdames J. Cornes, W. Scott, W. Cornes, A. Hesketh, W. Glover.

Members of Cronton Methodist Chapel pictured at the Pageant which was part of the Chapel's centenary celebrations in 1945.

In 1926 the Sunday School was altered and extended and to help pay for this work the Flower Show was inaugurated. This stayed a popular part of village life, the exhibition staying loyal and keeping the standard high, until about 1996 when sadly it ceased. The Chapel also once boasted a hockey team and a Brass Band. In 1945 to celebrate the

'The maypole' at the Pageant. Left to right: Joan Walmsley, Jenny Odgers, Dorothy Walmsley, Ann Walmsley, Blanche Crompton (May Queen), Janet Hewson, Joan Tyrer, Rouma Cornes, Ida Brimelow, Gwyneth Bellis, Barbara Odgers, Donald Burgess, Robin Glover Wendt.

"Temperance Group" at the Pageant. Back row: Dennis Cornes, Gladys Odgers, Maurice Wendt, Ella Hewson, Henry Stott, Marion Stott, Ken Marshall. Front Row: Helen Stott, Joyce Odgers, Doreen Beesley, Joan Bellis, Eva Hughes, Kathleen Odgers.

centenary a wide range of events took place and a cot was endowed in the National Children's Home in Frodsham. Every Christmas too there was carol singing round the main village by the Wesleyan Choir, always a delight.

The Chapel Room has always been full of life and at one time they used to give entertainments. These were very popular and well attended. Queues always formed outside. The Co-op also gave shows there and

Cronton Brass Band

afterwards they would give small gifts out such as packets of custard powder: all well received. I am indebted to the Methodist Chapel members for most of the above information.

Catholicism has always been strong in Cronton in common with elsewhere in the North West. As mentioned above Cronton Hall has a passage used by priests in penal times as an escape route. Thus the manor of Cronton must have been in Catholic hands at one time. As we all know the churches were taken over by the 'new' religion and Catholics and others were forced to attend service in the Anglican churches. Failure to do so resulted in fines. In 1641 three Cronton recusants were fined four shillings. No doubt services took place secretly here as elsewhere and as always there were informers. In 1910 the Stapleton-Bretherton family gave a church to Cronton (along with churches in Rainhill, Ditton and Widnes). It was built by Mr Joseph Mercer of Hough Green. Unfortunately the first pews, made of specially chosen seasoned oak, were burned in a fire at the builders yard supposedly started by dottle from one of the workmen's pipes. They had to be replaced by pine, which are lovely but not as good as oak. Holy Family Church was never completed. It lacks a tower on the south side of the door. The stained glass window on the right of the altar (made of Carara marble) depicts a soldier and a nun, members of the Stapleton-Bretherton family. In 1960 on August 15th a stained glass window on the other side of the altar was unveiled to celebrate the Golden Jubilee of the church. The church was redecorated for the

Fancy Dress, Holy Family Church Field Day, Pattens Orchard, Town End

occasion and the whole parish celebrated at a dinner. The first Priest was Father Joseph Commalach, later Dean, who served for many years. The first baby baptised there was Robert Frederick Atherton, born 26th August 1910 and baptised on 4th September. The first wedding was that of James Henry Glover and Alice Summner on 7th October 1911.

The Catholic church held an annual Gala Day until quite recently. These were well attended and special buses were put on for those people from Widnes who wished to attend. It was quite a village occasion. There was a fancy dress parade around the village, led by a band from Liverpool, side shows, races etc. One year there was an innovation: a Baby Show. This was quickly forgotten. It proved disastrous! The mothers who did not win argued and accused the winning baby of being older than the mother stated.

Christmas Tree

For the last few years an annual village Carol Service has been held in the church and proves immensley popular. In May 1924 Holy Family held a May Festival. It had a printed programme with the Latin heading,

"Deo Adjuvante Prosit Cronton" (God helping may Cronton prosper)

May Festival Programme - Front Cover

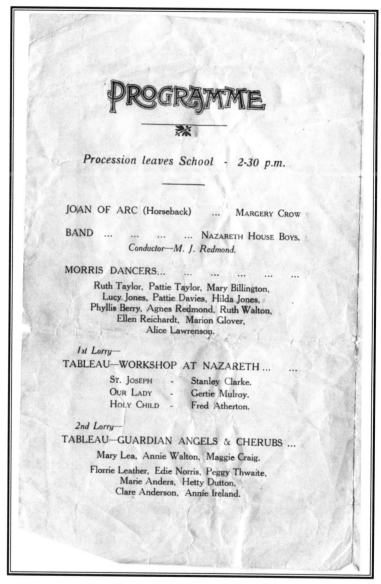

PROGRAMME

Procession leaves School - 2-30 p.m.

JOAN OF ARC (Horseback) ... MARGERY CROW

BAND ... ... NAZARETH HOUSE BOYS.
Conductor—M. J. Redmond.

MORRIS DANCERS... ... ...
Ruth Taylor, Pattie Taylor, Mary Billington,
Lucy Jones, Pattie Davies, Hilda Jones,
Phyllis Berry, Agnes Redmond, Ruth Walton,
Ellen Reichardt, Marion Glover,
Alice Lawrenson.

1st Lorry—
TABLEAU—WORKSHOP AT NAZARETH ... ...
ST. JOSEPH - Stanley Clarke.
OUR LADY - Gertie Mulroy.
HOLY CHILD - Fred Atherton.

2nd Lorry—
TABLEAU—GUARDIAN ANGELS & CHERUBS ...
Mary Lea, Annie Walton, Maggie Craig.
Florrie Leather, Edie Norris, Peggy Thwaite,
Marie Anders, Hetty Dutton,
Clare Anderson, Annie Ireland.

May Festival Programme - Inside

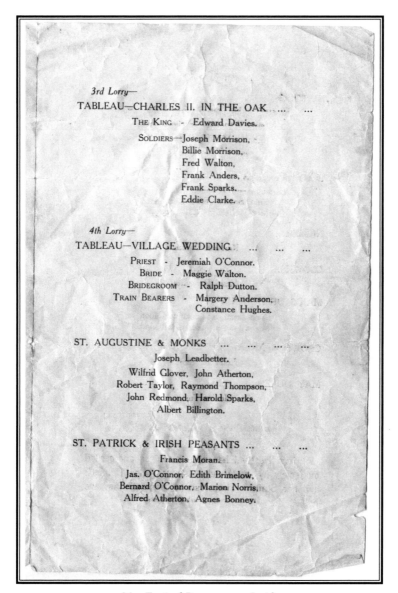

3rd Lorry—

TABLEAU—CHARLES II. IN THE OAK ... ...

THE KING - Edward Davies.

SOLDIERS—Joseph Morrison,
Billie Morrison,
Fred Walton,
Frank Anders,
Frank Sparks.
Eddie Clarke.

4th Lorry—

TABLEAU—VILLAGE WEDDING ... ...

PRIEST - Jeremiah O'Connor.
BRIDE - Maggie Walton.
BRIDEGROOM - Ralph Dutton.
TRAIN BEARERS - Margery Anderson,
Constance Hughes.

ST. AUGUSTINE & MONKS ... ...

Joseph Leadbetter.

Wilfrid Glover, John Atherton,
Robert Taylor, Raymond Thompson,
John Redmond, Harold Sparks,
Albert Billington.

ST. PATRICK & IRISH PEASANTS ... ...

Francis Moran.

Jas. O'Connor, Edith Brimelow,
Bernard O'Connor, Marion Norris,
Alfred Atherton, Agnes Bonney.

May Festival Programme - Inside

HUNTERS ... ...
MASTER OF HOUNDS - Fred Pilkington.
Monica Brandreth, Mollie Ireland,
Josephine Taylor, Gertie Ireland,
Olive Dutton, May Morrison,
Agnes Callon, Elizabeth Keavney.

PONY DANCERS ... ...
Bartholomew O'Connor, Alec. Thwaite,
Edith Sparks, Ellen Leadbetter,
Monica Ireland, Lily Edwards.

NIGGER... ... ...
Kenneth Davies.

CLOWN ... ...
Alfred Reichardt.

MAIDS OF HONOUR ... ...
Doris Brimelow, Beatrice Callon,
Mollie Glover, Eileen Redmond.

CROWN BEARER ... ...
Louis Redmond.

MAY QUEEN ... ...
Monica Taylor.

This Festival has been organized and carried
out solely by the Head Mistress, Miss Dennett,
and her Staff. They wish to thank all who have
helped them in any way whatsoever.

May Festival Programme - Back

There is no record why it was staged and I have not heard of any more festivals. It covered various subjects which don't seem to have any bearing on each other. Why did Joan of Arc lead the procession? I haven't been able to find out what pony dancers were. Did they belong to the hunt or were they a kind of dancing like the Morris Dancers? No-one can tell me.

Cronton was part of Farnworth and Anglicans went to Farnworth Church. However under a list of public services in 1876 it was recorded that a cottage lecture was given weekly in Cronton. The cottage is thought to have been the 'Little Cronton School' which was used later for services and entertainment in Cronton (also known as School House). Miss Longton of Cronton Hall gave the parish an American organ to help with their services and this was much appreciated. In 1880 Bible class started on Monday evenings, previously Protestant children joined the Wesleyan children in the chapel. In April 1907 after many problems and false starts the new Mission Hall was completed. It was built on land donated by the Park Family and funded by subscriptions. One donation came from a Mr Sharple, from a cotton mill in Shanghai, China.

A service was held on April 17th led by Canon Wright Williams, the Lord Bishop of Liverpool, who read special dedication prayers and preached the sermon.

Donors were:

The site:	The Park Family
Room:	The Park Family
Holy Communion Vessell	Mr & Mrs Neil
Holy Table	The Vicar
Brass Rail & Communicant Kneeler	Mr & Mrs C Wood
Linen for Holy Table	Mrs Wood
Reading Desk	Mrs Glover
	(in memory of the late Mr Glover)
Bible & Prayer Book for Reading Desk	A Friend
Chairs for Congregation	Miss M Riding
Kneeling Pads for Congregation	Miss Riding

Extensions were made in 1922 and 1926. An extra piece of land was given as a gift from Mrs Mary Cook in January 1937.

Services are now held in the Church of England School Room in Smithy Lane and we have our own Minister. On Sunday, 20th April 1997 at 10.30am the 90th Anniversary Service was held. The preacher was the Ven. Bob Metcalf, Archdeacon of Liverpool.

Hopefully the church will continue to grow and the centennial celebrations will be even greater. The Ecclesiastical Parish Boundary runs through Cronton, thus some of the Anglicans belong to the St Michael's parish in Hough Green.

At one time as in other parishes it was an annual event to 'beat the bounds'. The villagers walked around the boundary with the Ministers and small boys were beaten at intervals to instil into their minds knowledge of the parish boundaries. A few years ago Rev William Broad of St Michael's Hough Green walked the bounds of his parish. He was entertained to a lunch along with his other co-walkers at the Church of England School by the Parish Council. Please note that no small (or big) boys were beaten on this occasion.

Chapter 5:

Notable Cronton Men

Richard Wright

Some years ago a notebook was found in Cronton Hall written by Richard Wright whose family lived there. It starts in 1713 and ends in 1756. It is written on 'antique laid paper of Dutch manufacture', had parchment covers and formerly had a clasp. It measures three inches by four and three quarter inches and was written from each end. Richard Wright was obviously a rich man, he made loans to other people. He married his wife Mary, according to the notebook, on 27th July 1732. His daughter Sarah was christened on 2nd November 1734 at Warrington Parish Church. His occupation was given as Watchmaker. He was the son of Thomas Wright and his wife Jane Clayton. The Wrights had had Cronton Hall for generations until they sold it in 1821 to Bartholomew Bretherton.

An entry in the pocket book is for rent to Mr Norfolk for the sum of 5/- (25p) for a workshop described as *"a two pairs of stairs room"*. This indicated a room on the third storey where the light would be good - very essential for the fine work.

Work was also carried out on clocks as well as watches as evidenced by an entry for Thomas Birch. The most interesting entries relate to his work for London watchmakers. One of the first entries was for work

for Mr Goode. Between December 1713 and March 1715 he sold 23 movements (nearly 2 per month) costing around £1. 15.0d (£1.75p). Mr Goode was Charles Goode of the Strand, London who was made a freeman of the Clockmakers Company in 1686.

Other entries are for work for Mr Horseman between May 1721 and October 1722. These movements were numbered and can be traced to Quare & Horseman. Stephen Horseman was made a freeman of the Clockmakers Company in 1709 and went into partnership with Daniel Quare in 1718 and continued the business after Quare died in 1724. (Daniel Quare & Barlow invented the repeater).

The watches made by Quare & Horseman were numbered 4677 to 5503. Richard Wright's work was on numbers 5034, 5046, 5050, 5064, 5074, 5076, 5079, 5099, 5107, 5117, 5133, 5134, 5173, and 5178. Watches were sent to London to be finished, but some of Richard Wright's entries refer to watches being sent to him to be finished which was unusual and shows him to be a master of his craft.

Richard Wright did not send to Prescot for his work to go to London as did other makers in Cronton. One entry reads:
"Dec ye 4th 1723 sent per John Rigby to be delivered at ye Bell in Wood Street. Dec ye 12th 2 movements. Work for Mr Ellicot." (An illustration of the Bell in Wood Street appears in Plate 1 of William Hogarth's *"A Harlot's Progress"*, printed in 1723 nine years later than Richard Wright used it). Wright also used Thomas Aderson, Andrew Fearnough, Robert Fox, John Rigby, William Whitney and John Wood as carriers. He sent under the responsibility of named individuals and not on the coach from Warrington. They went to John Ellicot, a famous name for watchmaking, noted as an *"ingenius watchmaker of great note"*.

On August 10th 1724 he received from Mr Ellicot, a telescope costing 5/- (25p). The fact that John Ellicot (jnr) became outstanding in horological matters, was watchmaker to the King and was elected Fellow of the Royal Society seems to show that the Ellicots, father and son, were interested in astronomy as well as clock and watchmaking. The Wright family also shared this interest. Robert Wright of Winwick

wrote a book in 1727 entitled *'Lunar Tables, Motions etc'*, and in 1728 another entitiled *'Longtitude: By The Lunar Method'*.

The book of lunar tables contains a list of subscribers which included, 'Richard Wright of Cronton, Gent', and several others of the Wright family. Thomas was Richard's father. All together Richard Wright worked for seven London clock and watchmakers, all freemen of the Clockmakers Company and all were eminent in their trade.

The Worrell Family

Another important family in toolmaking was the Worrell family which spanned three generations in Cronton. The first was Thomas Worrell who after an argument with his father came to Cronton to work. He was born in Allerton in 1834. As he grew up he started helping his father with the farm. He really wanted to be a watchmaker and eventually his father agreed to apprentice his son to Webster of Aigburth. When another apprentice won promotion instead of Thomas he left Webster's. He came to Cronton to work for a watchmaker named James Wilcock. James kept the beerhouse called the 'Beehive'. In 1853 he fell in love with his employer's daughter Mary and they were married. Soon after he heard of a vacancy in Liverpool Postal Staff. He applied and got the job. Liverpool only had 115 postmen then and the office was in Canning Place. With only one delivery a day, he could fill the rest of his time mending clocks and watches. After a time he became a postman in Cronton. He stood in the road taking letters and the single penny for the stamp.

With his repairs and post work he had soon saved enough money to build his own house. With a friend he built his house with a workshop at the back. It is the house next to where the Smithy stood (now part of the Chip Shop) opposite the Post Office. It was he who suggested that there should be a Post Office in Cronton. It was agreed and he carried on that business from his house whilst still toolmaking.

When the Atlantic cable was laid from Britain to America in 1858 he was asked to make six pairs of clippers which were used to cut the cable as it was laid. When he received the order he was given a sample of the cable so that the clippers could be tested. One pair of clippers were faulty so it was kept as a family heirloom. After the test he extracted the copper wire from the cable and made souvenir pins and studs. These he polished and sold to the villagers to be kept in memory of the great event.

A very talented man, he wrote poetry for special occasions. He was an elocutionist and gave recitations. He was the 'wise man' and was called on for settling disputes. He had his own gas plant in the garden to supply his workshop long before Cronton received gas fron Widnes Corporation. When still in his twenties he was elected 'Mayor of Cronton' at a village festival. He died in 1916.

The second generation was Louis Worrell (Lou) born in 1868. He did not wish to follow his father's trade, he wanted to be a joiner. He gave in to his father and became a toolmaker. Competition from cheap machine tools had a detrimental effect, but when the First World War created trench warfare and a high demand for barbed wire there was a resulting increase in demand for wire cutters. Cronton's craftsmen had more work than they could handle. Lou like his father was multi-talented. With the help of his daughter Lydia, he ran the village Post Office. Sam Ireland, the postman, brought the letters from Prescot on his cycle and Lydia delivered them.

Lou was an accomplished pianist, playing at the Brick Wall Inn in Tarbock and for local dances. When Cronton celebrated the end of the First World War he played in the paviliion on Pex Hill. He bought a horse and cab and catered for weddings and christenings and took passengers to the railway stations at Rainhill, Farnworth and Hough Green. With the arrival of Widnes Corporation buses he went out of business. He died in 1947.

The third generation was Thomas Worrell who was born in 1904. He began his apprenticeship in toolmaking aged thirteen. He worked in the

workshop at the back of his grandfather's house in Cronton. He was a devoted craftsman. In the 1930s there was a decline in toolmaking in Cronton. Mass produced pliers and cutters replaced the handmade tools. Old craftsmen died or retired and no one took their places. So Thomas Worrell became the only toolmaker in the village. He continued his work by exporting, his tools going far and wide to places like Venezuela and Iraq. He also did work for colleges who needed tools for cane and leather work. When he died in 1973 he left behind pliers unfinished. The contents and equipment of his workshop are reconstructed at Prescot Museum.

Charles Leadbetter

Chartles Leadbetter was our local boy who made good. He was born in a small cottage next to Field House in 1681. His father John was a sundial maker, his mother was Katherine. Charles was the youngest of four brothers. He was baptised at Farnworth Church on September 8th 1861. His father died five years later leaving Katherine to bring up three sons (two children had died as babies). Charles lived in Cronton for 26 years and became a very clever man. It is not known where he received his education but there were two Grammar Schools in the vicinity, one at Farnworth and the other at Prescot. A clue as to how he was educated can be found in the preface to his book *'The Young Mathematician's Companion'.*

"Most people now in this age have an ambition of giving their children the best education that they can, and truly if I might advise, when youth has attained reading and writing good English, let him be put to the Mathematical school. But if the ability of the parent be in so low circumstances that they cannot afford it, then let them buy this book and the boy by his own genius may come at what will please the mind and not only that but make him capable of making satisfaction to the parent for the expense they have been at for his own improvement."

It appears that as a child he must have seen his father work on the sundials because in a later book he wrote, *'Merchanick Dialling or the*

True Art of Shadows', and goes into great detail about sundial making. In chapter four he describes, *"An erect declining dial for Liverpool, Cronton or Warrington in Lancashire."* He supplied the information for the aspect of a house for which the dial was made.

The figures quoted were facing 21° 10' West of South in Latitude 53° 22' North. Every building in Cronton was examined and none came near the above measurements until by the side of Field House, ruins of a small cottage were found, just 30' x 14', with a collapsed roof. The aspect of the wall was 21° W of S. The construction of a sundial was a complicated geometrical affair depending on whether it is to be horizontal or vertical, or any intermediate plane, inclined to the south or any angle between east and west. Charles Leadbetter provided a simplified account of it in his 'Mechanick Dialling'. At 26 years of age he wanted change and applied for training in the Customs and Excise Service. To do this he had to get a certificate from the Minister of the Parish where he was born. It had to certify that he was between 21 and 30 years of age, and if married have no more than two children. He also had to get a recommendation from a local gentleman. He was accepted and given over to training to William Hailwood of Prescot Outride (ie. The circuit of a guager on horsback round the town and villages in his own area) At 27 he was able to apply for his own outride. Here he had difficulty. A piece of advice in his book, *'The Royal Gauger'* states, *"And after all other steps have been taken, yet if the petitioner cannot obtain the countenance of some gentleman (a Member of Parliament is best) that is personally acquainted with one of the Commission frequently to solicit and remind the Commissioner of his promise, his petition will certainly come to nothing; for notwithstanding there are several vacancies either by deaths, discharges etc, happening every week and yet there are so many constantly applying, that those petitioners who have the best solicitors always succeed soonest".*

He was appointed first as a supernumerary in the Worcester collection. Shorly after he was promoted and became a gauger for a division called Bromsgrove "nd Outride. The industries he examined were tanneries, hop plantations, starch manufacuturers, soap and candlemakers, papermills, maltsters and victuallers. In August 1713 he was

discharged from the service after a dispute with a fellow officer, Thomas Brookes. Charles received a letter telling him he was discharged and despite his explanation of a misunderstanding he stayed discharged. He decided he would teach Mathematics, Astronomy and Navigation for which he was well qualified. He went to Shoreditch and set himself up under the sign of 'The Hand and Pen'. His advertisement read: *"Arts and Sciences, Mathematical; professed and taught by the author hereof at the Hand & Pen in Cock Lane, near Shoreditch, London, viz vulgar & decimal arithmatic, trigonometry, astronomy, surveying, gauging, dialling and navigation. Who also perform all sorts of measuring either for master or workman with care and expidition at reasonable rates"*

Near where Charles lived in Shoreditch there is a street called Little Britain which was full of publishers and here John Wilkinson of the Green Dragon published Charles Leadbetter's first book, *'A Treatise of Eclipses of the Sun & Moon'*. The motto on the title page translated from the Latin reads,*"The stars rule man, but God rules the stars"*. A poet friend George Nichols wrote this verse for the book,

"Great Cronton's Glory! Oh that I could raise
A monument might magnify they praise
But that's a Herculean task, ye thine
Own Works have done it, thus they piaises shine
Best from they own achievements; but lest I
Shadow the pariase with my obscuroty
I will be silent; let who will aspire
To speak they praise, rather I will admire
Thy matchless Arts; that makes thee soar so high
To know the language of the spangled sky;
God can resolve before we need to ask
When Sol puts on pale Luna's shady mask
You tell us of extremes both cold and hot
And when the Moon will wear a beauty spot;
The boundless skill with such unmated Glory
Hath crowned thy name, that's a living story
Of the great worth which may well be enroled
Not in paper but rich leaves of gold."

On the 21st April 1717 there was a Solar eclipse and in his eye witness account Charles Leadbetter says, *"This eclipse will be total in the middle counties but at Cronton in Lancashire, my native place, they will have a thread of light on the uperside of the sun...."* He replied to letters and queries but in his advert he advised, *"Those gentlemen that write are desired to pay the postage of their letters, or to expect no answer."*

He wrote in total eight books:

1. *A Treatise of Eclipses (1727)*
2. *Astronomy of the True System of the Planets (1727)*
3. *A Complete System of Astronomy*
4. *Astronomy of the Satellites of the Earth, Jupiter & Saturn (1729)*
5. *Uranoscopia, or The contemplation of the Heavens (1735)*
6. *Mechanick Dialling (1737)*
7. *The Royal Gauger (1739)*
8. *The Young Mathematician's Companion (1739)*

He died in 1744. Mr J. R. Platt, F.R.A.S. included all the above information and much more in his pamphlet, 'Charles Leadbetter, Cronton's Own Astronomer'. It is well worth reading.

Watchpart Makers & Tool Makers

Cronton was very famous for its tools and watchparts. They were considered very fine workmanship. Most of the houses in the village held workers and apprentices. Often a boy was put out to be apprenticed with another tool or watchpartmaker rather than learning from his own father. Careful study of the census rolls show this. Many farmers were also simultaneously involved in these trades. The wives of these craftsmen took in washing from the big houses in the neighbourhood, sometimes from as far afield as Liverpool. This petered out when the chemical industry came to Widnes. The prevailing wind from Widnes no longer brought clean drying air, but

filthy, greasy air which ruined the washing. Only in a few houses did the trade persist.

Most of the old cottages had workshops behind. The late Mr Neville Stott some years ago took Mr John Hunt B.A around the village to show him the cottages and workshops when Mr Hunt was writing his 'Toolmaking in Cronton'. Mr Hunt gave his notes to Mr Stott who gave them to me for this book. Mr F H Starkey M A also gave his help. The list they compiled whilst going round the village is as follows showing the toolmakers operating in 1925.

Ephram Glover: Penny Lane. He resided at the 'Bee Hive' public house and used the workshop of Mr Joe Anders for saw hardening.

Joseph Anders: Hand vice and pincers maker. His first workshop was in Smithy Lane after Brook Farm, (now demolished). As trade declined Mr Anders went to work in the chemical works in Widnes as a toolmaker. On retiring he set up business again in a workshop behind a small terrace of houses at 3, 5 and 7 Chapel Lane.

Peter Critchley: Toolmaker, who had the adjoining four cottages to Joseph Anders.

Bob Taylor: Toolmaker

Ephram Glover: Not to be confused with person of the same name mentioned above.#

Thomas Worrell: See above

Mr Dwerryhouse: Watchmaker, worked behind Cronton Post Office.

John Glover: Toomaker, 437 Cronton Lane

Henry Glover: Toolmaker (Roundabout)

Jack Brimelow: Toolmaker, Pex Hill. This workshop was demolished after being struck by lightning some years ago. He had three sons two of whom had the use of Thomas Worrell's workshop when working on their own account. The third son, Arthur went to Berry's Toolmakers, Heath Road Ditton.

John Sparks: Maker of nailpliers. His workshop was behind 3, 5 and 7 Chapel Lane.

Edward Jones: Toolmaker. His workshop was in Chapel Lane next to the Methodist Chapel.

Thomas Manifold: Toolmaker of Chapel Lane. His workshop was at the end of what was known as 'Swindle Terrace'.

Mr Horridge: Toolmaker, next to Tom Manifold.

Mr Wilkinson: Watchtool and watchpart maker, of 8 Chapel Lane now known as Laburnum Cottage.

James Glover: A farmer and watchmaker of Holly Farm. When Princess Alexandra came to England to marry Edward VII the people of London gave her a watch. It was supplied by McCabe of London who ordered the movement from James Glover of Cronton. The movement had to be extra jewelled and where possible made of gold.

Thomas Wilkinson: Toolmaker, lived opposite the Tavern in Upton Lane.

Joseph and James Dwerryhouse: Upton Tavern, worked behind Cronton Post Office.

Joseph and James Dwerryhouse: Upton Tavern, worked behind
                               Cronton Post Office.

Mr Glover: Watchpart maker of Leigh House, Chapel Lane, later
                    moved to Bear's Paw. This house had a two-storey
                    workshop with a laundry below. The tools made
                    were files, hand vices, pliers, nippers, compasses,
                    dividing callipers, and saws. Men who worked as file
                    cutters often suffered from the dust settling on them.
                    This was known as Grinders Disease. They were also
                    subject to plumbage poisoning from the lead beds on
                    which the files were cut, leading to a slow painful
                    death in both cases. Cronton workers used Spetler
                    beds which were less harmful.

Lists of Wills at Chester also throw up some interesting names and
dates of Cronton men in the toolmaking trade.

William Smith   Watch toolmaker, Cronton 1736
George Birchall   Watchmaker Cronton 1761
William Garnett   Watchmaker Cronton 1785
George Elerby   Watch toolmaker Cronton

Old directories of Lancashire list the following in Cronton:

Slater's directory 1855

Toolmakers:
Peter Critchley   Thomas Leather
Ralph Dutton   Giles Smith
Edward Glover   John Smith
Ephram Glover   William Twigg
William Glover   James Wilcock
Henry Lowe   Richard Woodfall

Kelly's Directory 1864

Ralph Glover	Watch toolmaker
Edward Glover	Watch toolmaker
Ephram Glover	Watch toolmaker
George Glover	Watch toolmaker
George Glover	Watch fusee maker
John Glover	Watch wheel maker
John Hesketh	Watch barrel maker
George Lowe	Watch toolmaker
Henry Lowe	Watch toolmaker
James Smith	Watch toolmaker
John Smith	Farmer and toolmaker
James Wilcock (The Bee Hive)	Watch toolmaker and Beer Retailer

Slater's Directory 1895

Anders James	Smithy Lane Cronton - Hand Vices
Brandreth John	Chapel Lane Cronton
Critchley John	Smithy Lane Cronton
Dutton Henry	Cronton
Dutton William	Cronton
Dwerryhouse John	Warrington Road Cronton
French Joseph	Chapel Lane Cronton
Glover Ephram	Smithy Lane Cronton
Glover James	Smithy Lane Cronton
Glover Joseph	Warrington Road Cronton
Ireland William	Lodge Lane Cronton
Lowe George	Town End Cronton
Manifold Thos.	Chapel Lane Cronton
Smith John	Town End Cronton
Smith William	Smithy Lane Cronton
Sparks George	Chapel Lane
Wilkinson George	Chapel Lane Cronton
Worrell Thomas	Warrington Road Cronton

In a book by a Mr E. Surey Dane entitled, *'Peter Stubbs and the Lancashire Hand Tool Industry'*, he lists toolmakers working at home. Those from Cronton are listed as:

Appleton James Snr	Files	Cronton	1789
Appleton James Jnr	Files	Cronton	1789
Lowe George		Cronton	1815
Lowe Henry		Cronton	1807
Shaw James		Cronton	1822
Elaby Thomas		Cronton	1803
Glover John		Shears, pincers, pliers, tongs, turnbenches, scissors, saw blades	

Peter Stubbs was tenant of the White Bear Inn in Bridge Street, Warrington where he combined the activities of innkeeper, maltster, brewer and file maker, on a large scale.

Chapter 6:

The Parish Council

In 1894 the Local Government Act was passed which set up Rural and Urban District Councils. Rural Councils were allowed to have Parish Councils which took over some of the work of the Overseers, Constables and Surveyors of Highways. In 1896 Cronton Parish Council met for the first time. The earliest Minute book I can find starts in 1919. Mr James Leather was then the Chairman, and the other members were Messrs Collinson, Fairley, Jones and Pitt. The business was entirely taken up with trying to get better postal facilities for Cronton. Mr Taylor represented Cronton as District Councillor.

At first the councillors appeared to denigrate anything new. They would not have street lighting in Cronton, or scavenging (rubbish clearance!). I do not know why. In 1929 they refused to pay £10 to Widnes Fire Brigade. In retaliation Widnes Fire Brigade refused to attend fires in Cronton. The reason the council gave was that if there was a fire in Widnes and one in Cronton at the same time they didn't think Widnes would give the Cronton fire priorty despite the £10 fee (a month's wages for a labourer if he was lucky!).

The Clerk to the Council at first also had to collect the tithes on the land which was handed out to the poor and sick as alms, as had been the case since Elizabeth I had started the 'Vestries'. He spent a lot of time writing letters, first reminding the tithe payers that the tithes were due,

then overdue, then very outstanding and then demanding. His letters became sterner and more desperate as time went on! (It was the wealthier people who invariably held back their tithes).

In 1930 a boundary change was discussed. It was felt by the powers that be that Cronton had a greater affinity with Widnes than Whiston (we now had buses from Widnes). Cronton disagreed and decided to stay with Whiston, the loyalty of the Widnes Fire Brigade again being a factor. It was felt that Whiston Fire Brigade would arrive more quickly down the 'back lanes'. And after all Whiston was a rural district as opposed to Widnes which was an urban district. It was not felt that Widnes would understand rural matters.

In 1939 at the outbreak of World War II the council got new powers. They organised the LDV, the Local Defence Volunteers, subsequently known as the Home Guard. They trained each Sunday morning. The Air Raid Warden Post was in School House (where the Parish Council Offices were), and there was a smaller hut in Hall Lane for fire watching. They went about seeing that curtains were drawn and that no light was showing and that no one had lights on their cycles. They also gave out gas masks, spoke to the children in schools on what to do if we were under rubble in a bombed building (shout!). Children were told if a siren went when we were outside we were to walk - not run, which caused panic, to the nearest school, church or house if our own homes were too far away (in Cronton?). We were told that running killed more people than bombs. It all terrified me!

On a Sunday morning there was the practised shooting in the quarry and in the afternoon the boys collected the bullet shells. In the 'lulls' between bombings they played cards. One of the card players regularly lost all his money and then played for his horse. This too he regularly lost, but no one had the heart to take it (it was liable to bolt anyway).

In 1974 the Parish Council was allowed to increase its membership to 10 in view of the increased population. In 1990 we again faced a boundary decision - whether to stay with Knowlsey Council or go to Halton Borough Council. A lot of people, mostly newer residents, felt

Halton would treat us better, the older inhabitants again wanted the status quo. (In any case we received many secret messages from Widnes to say that they didn't want us because they had enough trouble of their own). Parish Councillors were beseiged whenever they left their homes. The Clerk's phone never stopped ringing. The village was in uproar. It was decided that the fairest way to decide things was by a Referendum. Halton Council were asked to address the village at a public meeting - they politely declined. Knowsley Council did and addressed a very acrimonious meeting. No progress at all was made. The referendum was held and by a small majority it was decided to stay with Knowsley. This it must be said, was a great relief to both Knowsley and Halton but the complaints rumbled on for years until Knowsley's rate dropped below Halton's and peace arrived.

In 1990 on Thursday November 6th our War Memorial was unveiled in memory of eleven Cronton men who went to war in WWI and WWII and who never returned. Some of the relatives still lived in the village. I was asked to try and find the relatives of the others who had moved away.

Accordingly, I put an advertisement in several papers and one night I received a letter from the niece of Charles Wright (named on the War Memorial) Eileen Short, who lived in Australia. She had received a copy of one of the advertisements. She gave me an address and telephone number for Chorley. I rang and spoke to a very old gentleman who was Charles Wright's brother. He had left Cronton years and years ago and asked where I lived. He was amazed to discover that I was living in the house where he himself had lived, and that his playfriend had been my father who then lived next door. He agreed to come to my home on the night the Memorial was unveiled to rest and wait for the ceremony. Unfortunately he became ill and was unable to attend. He died shortly afterwards. His daughter came as did Mrs Eileen Short, his niece, from Australia. They were very grateful for the work of the Parish Council and the people who had contributed the money. The ceremony was introduced by Mr J.H Reynolds, J.P. and unveiled by Cllr Mrs G Reynolds, Chairman of the Parish Council. Her speech was as follows:

"Ladies and Gentlemen, On behalf of the village of Cronton I am pleased to accept this Monument into the safe keeping of the Parish Council. Before the unveiling I would just like to say that I hope this memorial will be of some comfort to the relatives of these gallant men, to know that their bravery has at last been recognised and their supreme sacrifice was not in vain. A short while ago, I thought that 1990 was an ideal year for the completion of our own Memorial. It is the 50th anniversary of the Battle of Britain, the Berlin Wall came down and the super powers were starting to reduce weapons. But unfortunately the tension in the Gulf has placed our forces once more in the front line. Many of our fellow countrymen, women and children are still hostages in Iraq and Kuwait. I sincerely hope that a peaceful solution will soon be found. In future years perhaps, this memorial will be a constant reminder to all that war can never solve the problems of this world. Therefore in memory of all who gave their lives in the cause of freedom I will now unveil this memorial."

Afterwards there was a reception in the Community Centre for the village. It was greatly enjoyed. The memorial cost £3,000 and Knowsley Council allowed us to use the land sold by Mr Alexandra F.Farrell to Whiston RDC on 14th January 1937 for £90. The Council also provided the landscaping services. The stone came from Italy.

The Parish Council now meets in an office leased from Knowsley Council. We have had a great many good parish councillors but amongst the most hardworking and longest serving members I list:

Norman Ney	Parish and District Councillor
J H Reynolds	Parish and District Councillor
Geoff Sharples	Parish and District Councillor
K Sumner	Parish Councillor

Chapter 7:

Education in the Village

The Dame School at Cronton was one of the first in the area. It was opened at the house on the main road past the old cottages going towards the Black Horse. It was once two houses but is now one. The children attending took coal for the fire and a penny or twopence for lessons if their parents could afford it.

Margaret Wright paid 5/- (50p) for books for the school. She lived at Cronton Hall. Later on a school was opened at the Smith's house, now known as School House opposite the Mission Hall (Community

Holy Family School Circa 1912

Centre). In the early years of the 20th century a little girl attending the school was putting coal on the fire when her pinafore (which all little girls wore) caught fire. She threw her arms up to protect her face and caught her apron between them thus burning her face badly. She carried the scars for the rest of her life.

The Stapleton-Bretherton family built Holy Family School, which opened in 1893. It consisted of a small classroom and a much larger one, the end of which was separated by a screen and whose floor was higher. This was for a Church for Mass on Sundays. After the Church was built it was used as an extra classroom. The classrooms were heated by coal fire. In the winter when it was very cold we could pull our desks round the fire, which was lovely. The boys put the coal on the fire. My grandmother cleaned the school each night and I would lift the chairs in the little class on to the tables. She would come in and brush up and dust and I would put the chairs down again. She came in early in the morning to start all the fires.

The ink we used was made by the boys on Friday afternoon from powder and water. The girls washed the inkwells. Sometimes the ink was like porridge and other times so thin our exercise books looked as though a spider had crawled across them. This always inflamed the Headteacher! It usually took two tries to get it right. There were two cloakrooms. One for the girls and the 'babies' and one for the big boys.

The cane was very prominent in the 'big boys' class and was used regularly on all of us. Sometimes I got it but didn't know what for. I can only imagine it was for laughing or talking. On Friday afternoons the big girls cleared out the teacher's room. Tea leaves (kept all week) were spread on the carpet and them brushed off it. We polished the chairs and table and cleaned the stove. Then it was 'inspected'. If not up to the mark we started again. It had a detrimental effect on me - I still do not like housework.

At dinner time a girl was chosen to lay the table with knife and fork and napkin for the teacher's dinner. We made tea and warmed up dinners (pies, stews in bottles etc) for children who lived too far to go home.

During the war we had gas mask drill when at some part of the day we had to wear our masks whilst we worked. I noticed the teachers never suffered the awful practice. The boys of course made horrible noises in their masks and denied any knowledge of doing it. They got caned and we got caned for giggling at the noise. We had an air raid shelter which was a dug out on the school field. We went down to practise and also when the sirens went.

Empire Day was celebrated by marching in the playground as was Oak Apple Day (in remembrance of King Charles hiding in the oak tree). The boys got long nettles and nettled the legs of girls not wearing oak leaves. I was always terrified of Oak Apple Day. I always had oak leaves as did the other children but they were rudely snatched off and we were nettled anyway. We had a Christmans party and 'danced' around the room...the dance went a heel a toe (stamped on the floor) and a 1 2 3 (we took three steps) - whilst the teacher thumped a tune on the piano! We did it in pairs with crossed hands. I was always glad when it was finished. We made paper chains by the mile which were put up in the classrooms. That I did like. For several years a local man bought us all a present which was delivered by Father Christmas.

We also had a May and June procession when we walked around the Church. We had to make blue headdresses (ribbons made into flowers) for May and red headdresses for June. We wore white dresses and veils. It was a good school but I hated it and was glad to leave. Until 1930 the Anglican and Methodist children attended the school.

They got their own school in 1930 on the land given for the Mission Church. Most of the children left the Catholic school and went to the new school. I am grateful to Mr and Mrs Henry Stott for a copy of the first registers. I do not know much about this school but it certainly turned out good scholars. I asked several of the early pupils for their memories but all they could remember was the cocoa, which Mrs Norris the caretaker, came in to make for them on cold days when they played in the playground during the winter. They loved her for that!

CRONTON C.E SCHOOL 1944 JUNIORS
Back Row (left to right): Mrs Norris, caretaker, ? Almond, Ian Dutton,
Unknown , Unknown , Carlton Patton, Miss Ratcliffe, headteacher.

Middle Row: Eric Bott, Unknown, Roma Cornes, Ida Brimelow, Norma
Dutton, Hilda Parker, Unknown,, Brian Preston, Frank Winstanley.

Front Row: Unknown, Rhoda Smith, Unknown, Betty Houghton, Pat Walker,
Beryl Glendenning, Margaret Teeling, Norma Garner.

However, I have received the following from Muriel Brown (nee Garner) who was a pupil during the 1930s: *"Mrs Norris was caretaker when I was there. Every morning she made us chocolate Horlicks and we had little mugs with nursery rhyme characters on the front. We all wanted Tom Mix as there was only one of those. The field the group is sitting in was donated by Mr Cook, father of Fred and Nancy, who lived opposite the school. My teachers were Miss Goulding and Miss Baldwin, who used to gossip at the bus stop with Miss Mooney and Mrs Redmond from Holy Family School. About 1936/37 Mr Merriman (Tommy Merriman, bookmaker) won the Irish Sweepstake - £15,000 I believe; a huge sum then. He built a house at the bottom of Pex Hill Avenue and his children went to Holy Family. He was a most generous man, and as well as giving all the children at Holy Family a Christmas gift, he gave them to us as well."*

The old Catholic school has gone and a new bigger one takes its place. The Anglican school is now used as a Comunity Centre and a big new one stands in Smithy Lane. I delight in going into this school each year to talk to some of the children about 'old' Cronton when I was at school! Both schools continue with loyal service to the community. I did try to find out more about both schools from scholars, particularly about unsusual happennings but we must have been a dull lot; no-one could remember anything!

One headteacher, years ago, showed me the school log book for the Church of England School. The only thing we thought worth mentioning was the fact that on one Grand National Day, long gone, when the school was on the 'main road', the then Head Teacher closed the school for the day because he felt the traffic could be heavy through the village. To Aintree? This was a rough road at a time when very few people had cars! I think he or she was into heavy betting.

Headteachers of Holy Family R.C. Primary School

Mrs M Dennett	1893 - 1925	32 years
Miss Smith	1926 -1928	1.5 years
Miss Mooney	1928 - 1951	23 years
Miss Devereux	1952 -1953	1.5 years
Mrs M Shawcross (Rotheram)	1953 -1976	23 years
Mr J Martin	1977 - 1980	3.5 years
Miss T Kenna	1980 - 1997	17 years
Mrs C Hamilton	1997 - 2001	4 years
Mrs Cook-Hannah	2002	

Finale

The village started to be enlarged (housewise) in the early 1960s. Life didn't change for the villagers. We met new people but that had happened before and they were all accepted and 'fitted in'. Most Cronton people had, for generations, possibly back to Adam, married 'outsiders' and they all settled in. Contrary to what has been said to me often, we do not have any animosity towards new villagers. What we do regret is the loss of lovely trees, hedges and woods, and the lovely cornfields and the open spaces where we could see forever. At night we could hear the porter at Farworth Station shouting to the approaching train "Farnworth", and St Paul's clock chiming at midnight.

With the loss of hedges and fields we lost birds; larks, plovers, lapwings, owls, swifts and swallows who came in their hundreds in Spring and left in Autumn. Kingfishers flew along the stream (which had a lovely sandy bottom and was clean) to catch the Jacksharps which changed to beautiful colours in the breeding season. Newts swam in the stream. We miss the field mice (increasing again), the voles, lizards, frogs, toads and horses (clopping along the road) and the pigs, hens, ducks, and proud magnificent geese.

We were well endowed with mushrooms and blackberries, which I love, and which kept us in jam during the war. We miss the flowers, the Red Campion, Periwinkles, Eye Bright, Star of Bethlehem, Sun Spurge,

Meadow Sweet, Corncockle, Cranesbill, Stitchwort, Ox-Eyed Daisy, and most important of all, Scarlet Pimpernell, which told us whether it would be fine or rainy.

We miss the 'Orchard Pit', a deep pond for skating on in Winter and the lanes to sledge along. We miss the farms and their barns, with their lovely smell, the haystacks and the Smithy. We remember also those who came to help on the farms for the harvests. There were pea pickers, potato pickers, Irish labourers for the grain harvest. Italian prisoners of war kept the brook clear and included a young man who sang arias and was studying at la Scala Milan. He had been told to surrender to the British at the earliest opportunity to make sure his voice was saved. And of course there were the gypsies. Most of all I remember the tramp who lived in the barn at Town End. A quiet, gentle man who had lost his spirit in the war. The Town End cottagers made him breakfast in turn each day: toast, bacon and an egg. We were rewarded by blackberries or a few dry sticks for the fire. When Hall Lane was developed he said goodbye. It was a slower way of life (but we still knew stress!). But now we do have more friends, more company and more people to worry about and help. We do not resent your presence but like everyone else we would like what we have lost as well, as you would too if you had known it.

We hope Cronton continues as a village for a long time and that you too contribute to the ongoing history. My good wishes to you all who read my 'book' and thank you for my lovely life in Cronton.

Appendix One
Coronation Programme

Ye Olde Township of Cronton

CORONATION
CELEBRATIONS

Programme

of Events ..

At
Pex Hill,

JUNE 22nd, 1911.

Members of Cronton Parish Council:

Mr. THOMAS WORRALL, Chairman.

Mr. G. H. WEBSTER, Vice-Chairman.

Councillors :

Mr. WM. ALMOND.   Mr. G. WILKINSON

Mr. J. LEATHER.   Mr. F. HERRIMAN

Mr. E. J. JACKSON (Clerk).

EDWARDS, PRINTER, WIDNES

PROGRAMME.

12-30 to 1 o'clock,

School Children to leave Cronton Village and walk in procession to Pex Hill.

1-50 to 2-0.

40 yards race for Girls 3 to 5 years.
First Prize 1/, Second 6d., Third 3d.

First   Second   Third

2-0 to 2-5.

40 yards race for Girls 3 to 5 years.
First Prize 1/-, Second 6d., Third 3d.

First   Second   Third

2-5 to 2-10.

60 yards race for Girls 3 to 5 years.
First Prize 1/-, Second 6d., Third 3d.

First   Second   Third

2-10 to 2-15.

60 yards race for Boys 3 to 5 years.
First Prize 1/-, Second 6d. Third 3d.

First   Second   Third

2-15 to 2-55.

Entertainment by Scholars of Holy Family School.

Part 1

Chorus....................... "Rule Britannia"
Senior Boys and Girls.

Dance .... "Gavotte"
Infants.

Song................................. "Posies"
Junior Girls.

Country Dance .... "16th Century"
P. Walton, Ethel Taylor, H. Atherton, Nancy Glover,
F. Sparkes, Nellie Glover.

Song.................... "Ladies and Gentlemen"
Infants.

Chorus............. "Flow on thou shining river"
Senior Boys and Girls.

3-0 to 3-5.

80 yards race for Boys 8 to 11 years.
First Prize 1/6, Second 1/-, Third 6d.

First   Second   Third

3-5 to 3-20.

½ mile flat race, age 14 and over.
First Prize 3/-, Second 2/-, Third 1/-.

First   Second   Third

3-20 to 3-25.

80 yards race for Girls 8 to 11 years.
First Prize 1/6, Second 1/-, Third 6d.

First   Second   Third

3-25 to 3-30.

100 yards race for Boys 8 to 11 years.
First Prize 1/6, Second 1/-, Third 6d.

First   Second   Third

_____

3-30 to 3-35.

100 yards race for Girls 8 to 11 years.
First Prize 1/6, Second 1/-, Third 6d.

First   Second   Third

_____

3-35 to 3-40.

100 yards race for Girls 12 to 15 years.
First Prize 1/6, Second 1/-, Third 6d.

First   Second   Third

_____

3-40 to 3-45.

100 yards race for Boys 12 to 15 years,
First Prize 1/6, Second 1/-, Third 6d.

First   Second   Third

_____

3-45 to 5-0.

Tea for children and old persons 55 years and up.

_____

5-10 to 5-50.

Children of Holy Family School.

Part 2.

Chorus............................ "King's Navy"
Senior Boys and Girls.

Song......................."Grandmothers Old"
Junior Girls.

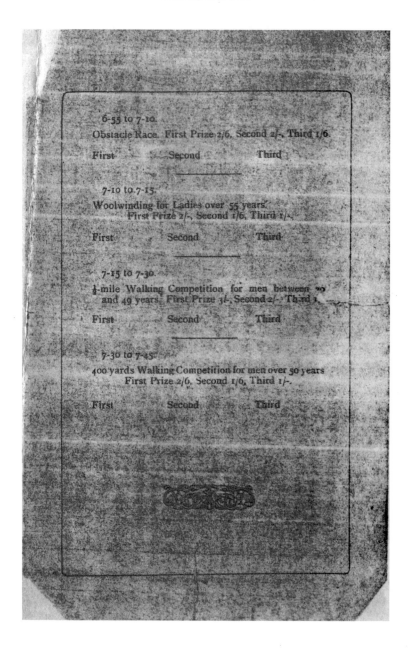

6-55 to 7-10.

Obstacle Race. First Prize 2/6. Second 2/-. Third 1/6.

First   Second   Third

_____

7-10 to 7-15

Woolwinding for Ladies over 55 years.
First Prize 2/-, Second 1/6, Third 1/-.

First   Second   Third

_____

7-15 to 7-30.

½-mile Walking Competition for men between 40
and 49 years. First Prize 3/-, Second 2/-, Third 1/-

First   Second   Third

_____

7-30 to 7-45.

400 yards Walking Competition for men over 50 years
First Prize 2/6, Second 1/6, Third 1/-.

First   Second   Third

7-45 p.m.

IN THE PAVILION.

CONCERT by
Messrs. Firth's & Phillips' Party

Part 1.

Pianoforte Selection .... _____
Miss Davies.

Song........................ "Long live the King"
Mr. Nausen.

Humorous Song .... _____
Mr. D. Broome.

Coon Song and Dance........................ _____
Mr. E. Firth.

Song .... _____
Mr. H. Firth

Comic Song and Dance .... _____
Mr. C. Firth.

Song .... _____
Mr. F. Phillips.

Interval of 5 minutes.

Part 2.

Messrs. Firth and Phillips and Company present
their Speciality Sketch, entitled

'Coronation Celebrations in Old Kentucky'

by a few of His Majesty's subjects.

During the sketch they will introduce high-class
Solos, Duetts, Trios, clever and up-to-date Sand
Dancing, Clog Dancing, Boot Dancing, Bone
Selections and other musical items.

Accompanist Miss Davies

10-15 to 12-30 a.m.

DANCING to Pitt and Worrall's Band.

God Save the King.

Sports Committee:

Chairman : REV. H. NORMAN BACHE.
MESSRS. W. KERRY, J. WELSBY, J. FAIRLEY,
J. CLARKE, R. BOWERMAN, F. GLOVER,
A. HOUGHTON, H. HOUGHTON.

Handicappers : R. BOWERMAN, F. GLOVER,
J. FAIRLEY.

Starter : JOHN WELSBY.

Stewards : J. CLARKE, A. HOUGHTON,
H. HOUGHTON.

Judges : REV. H. NORMAN BACHE, W. KERRY.
Blue Rosettes.

Entertainment Committee:

Chairman : MR. F. HERRIMAN
MESSRS G. WILKINSON, W. CORNES, W.
WYCHERLEY, F. COLLINSON, J. LEA,
J. ISON, W. HOUGHTON, T. COOK,
E. PITT, J. GLOVER, Senr., R. JOHNSON,
J. GLOVER, Junr., JOHN GLOVER.
White Rosettes.

Refreshment Committee:

Chairman : MR. W. GLOVER.
MESSRS. T. WORRALL, E. PITT, E. HEWSON,
JAMES GLOVER, W. ROBINSON,
JAS. COOK.
Red, White and Blue Rosettes.

Ladies Committee:

MESDAMES. WELSBY, TAYLOR, HEWSON,
T. WORRALL, COOK, M. A. GLOVER,
PITT, A. HOUGHTON (T.E.), H. GLOVER,
Wm. FRANCE, ANDERS, HARGREAVES,
A. GLOVER, DENNETT, A. HOUGHTON,
BRANDRETH, R. GLOVER, T. GLOVER,
CORNES.
Red White and Blue Rosettes.

Chairman of General Committee : REV. FATHER
KELLY.—*Purple and White Rosette.*

Secretary and Treasurer : MR. E. J. JACKSON.
White Rosette with Streamers.

Appendix Two
Holy Family School Diary 1893-94
& Register Pages

1893 - 4

Dec. 3.   School opens with 47 children over 40 of which have been in attendance at Rainhill R. C. Schools.

  Staff.

   Margaret Dennett. C.T.

   Mary J. Cleary. Cand. for. Art. 68.
      age: 13. Ap. 1866

Dec. 8.   Thirteen admissions have been made during the week. Average attendance 54.

Dec. 15.   Visit from Rev. Manager on Wednesday.

Dec. 22.   School closes for Xmas. holiday.

Dec. 29.   Holiday

Jan. 5.   "

Jan. 12.   School reopened on Monday. Visit from Attendance Officer on Tuesday.

Jan. 19.   The infant room has this week been fitted with desks.

Jan. 26.   Visit from Mr. Collingwood on Monday.

1894. 2

Feb. 2. Notice received on Tuesday.
that the school will be
examined in the month of June

Feb. 9. Holiday was given on the
afternoon of the 5th it being
Shrove Tuesday – also on
Wednesday morning to
enable the children to
attend church.

Feb. 16. Attendance Officer visited
on Tuesday.

Feb. 23. List of <u>Object Lessons</u> for
Infant Class.

(1) Cotton. Silk.

(2) Coal, Salt, Gold.

(3) Horse, Dog, Cat. Hen & Chickens.

(4). Farmyard. Table & Chair,
Clock, Parts of a tree.

(5). Apple. Cocoa.

<u>Occupations.</u>

Class 1. Drawing. Figure laying.

" II. Mat weaving, Ravelling.
Bead threading.

NAME.	No.	NAME.
	286	Atherton Veronica
	307	Asche Anthony
	323	Atherton Winstan
43. Atherton, Fred.	324	Atherton David
60. Atherton Herbert	325	Atherton Alan
62. Atherton Henry.	342	Atherton Thomas
66. Anders Gladys.	351	Atherton Ann
75. Atherton Joseph.	402	Adamson, Mary
100. Atherton Willie	504	Atherton Mary Elizabeth
103. Atherton Thos.	513	Atherton, Pamela Josephine
	604	Atherton, Mark
	628	Arlquist, Bernadette Anne
Aldred Doris	664	Ashton, Henry
139. Aldred William	665	Ashton, Thomas
	666	Ashton, Brian
	667	Ashton, Joseph
26. Atherton Alfred	695	Alquist, Richard Benedict
5-1 Atherton John	705	Ashton, Carol
	707	Atherton, Angela
	708	Atherton, Andrew
72. Adams Bert.	719	Atherton, Susan Ann
74. Adams Eva	762	Atherton, Susan
7- Adams Ada	798	Appleton, Mark
78. Adams Edith	807	Atherton, David
19. Anders Frida	878	Atherton, Peter Eric
4 Anders Marie	885	Atherton, Simon Alfred
127 Anders Agnes	909	Atherton, Lynne Catherine
180 Atherton Thomas	958	Atherton, Helen Marie
191 " Eric	1004	Archibald, Andrew
230. " Winifred Maureen	1058	Archibald, John Paul
237 " John Alex	1090	Archibald, Christopher David
206 Atherton G. Margaret	1061	Aouadi, Rebecca Sarah (see LYNCH)
243 Atherton Norma Frances	1119	Aronson, Helen
245 Atherton Margaret Iris	1145	Armstrong Neil Edmund

No.	NAME.	No.	NAME
9	Brimelow Arthur	185	Burke Terence
		187	Burke Mary Hilda
		188	" Thora Margaret
		189	Berry Mary Lily
53	Bonney Mary 2.	197	Berry William
54	Bishop Priscilla	211	Beamond Geoffrey Hedly
58	Bonney Dorothy.	212	Broome Harry
64	Bonney Martha.	215	Brandreth Ronald
72	Bonney Annie.	226	" Frank
73	Brandreth John	236	Baker Allen
80	Brandreth Olive.	244	Brandreth Edgar
107	Brandreth Edgar	218	
		280	Brandreth John
		312	Brandreth Anthony
		327	Brandreth Margaret Rose
		270	Brandreth Maurice
	Blyth	354	Bingham John
	Brandreth Eleanor	367	Byrne Michael David
155	Brimelow Arthur	381	Buck, Kathleen Patricia
166	Brown James	391	Brough, Patricia
167	Brown Samuel	412	Byrne, Paul Christopher
168	Brown John	426	Brough, Eileen
169	Brown Annie	447	Boyle, Patricia
170	Bonney Margaret	451	Ackley, Kevin
4	Brandreth Eleanor	455	Barber, Pamela Jane
18	Brandreth Joseph	464	Burman, Janet Margaret
22	Bonney Annie	466	Brough, Michael
	Brandreth Monica	477	Brown, Susan
53	Brimelow Doris	481a	Byrne, Kevin
54	Brimelow Edith.	497	Burman, Frances
	Berry Phyllis	502	Craven, Francis
	Berry Mabel.	640	Burgess, William Henry
91	Booth Mary	645	Barnwell, Denise
99	Booth Nora	646	Barnwell, Karen

Appendix Three
Cronton C of E School
Admissions Register

No.	Admission Day	Month	Year	Name	Day	Month	Year
1	18	8	30	Adams Thomas	25	3	1924
2	"	"	"	Hunt Joseph	12	2	1925
3	"	"	"	Cook Fred	27	1	1926
4	"	"	"	Thompson Peter	25	2	1925
5	29.4.31	"	"	Critchley Austin Leonard	14	11	1923
6	"	"	"	Adams Elsie	7	2	1922
7	"	"	"	Collison Florence May	29	3	1921
8	"	"	"	Hunt Elizabeth Ellen (Dorothy)	21	7	1922
9	"	"	"	Hunt Elsie	13	12	1923
10	"	"	"	Thompson Eileen	6	3	1926
11	"	"	"	Thompson Kathleen	2	7	1921
12	"	"	"	Thompson Dorothy	30	1	1923
13	29.6.31	"	"	Critchley Winifred May	22	10	1921
14	"	"	"	Prescott John	11	2	1922
15	"	"	"	Prescott Dennis	25	8	1924
16	"	"	"	Whitfield James	11	3	1924
17		19	8	30	Prescott Henry	23	12	1919
18		20	8	30	Pitt William	15	2	1923
19	11.2.31	"	"	Pitt Edward Broch	21	5	1927
20		25	8	30	Berry Frederick Horace	24	4	1921
21	"	"	"	Collison Frederick John	29	9	1924
22	"	"	"	Lyons Robert	30	5	1924
23	"	"	"	Lyons Albert	6	5	1926
24	"	"	"	Pilkington George	1	1	1922
25	"	"	"	Reynolds Henry	5	7	1924
26	"	"	"	Harding Stanley	28	9	1925
27	15.11.30	"	"	Prescott Joyce Cox	7	1	1927
28	9.9.31	26	"	Harrison Henry Gordon Reynolds	3	1	1927
29	1	9	30	Harvey John	2	9	1922
30	9	9	30	Beesley Dorothy	24	10	1926
31	15	9	30	Harding Jack	13	8	1922
27	(Re admit) 11	11	30	Prescott Joyce Cox	7	1	1927
32	5	1	31	Whitfield Joyce	27	2	1922
33	5	1	31	Whitfield Gladys	21	1	1926
34	5	1	31	Winstanley Alan	20	2	1924
35	5	1	31	...rth Eva	18	2	"
				Alan	9	1	

PARENT OR GUARDIAN		FORMER SCHOOL	WITHDRAWAL			
Name	Address		Day	Month	Year	Cause
Adams Albert	Penny Lane Cronton	Whiston C.E.	18	4	35	Left District
Hunt Albert	" "	Holy Family	17	7	36	Farnworth C.
Cook Arthur	Penwood Farm "	None	16	7	37	Farnworth C.E
Thompson Peter	Council Houses Cronton	Holy Family	17	7	36	Farnworth C.
Critchley Louis	Smithy Lane "	"	20	10	30	Returned to 8 Yrs.
Adams Albert	Penny Lane "	Whiston C.E.	26	8	33	Ht Farnworth attending
Collison Frank	Town End "	Farnworth C.E	13	7	32	Farnworth C.E
Hunt Albert	Penny Lane "	Holy Family	21	7	33	Ht Whiston Cen
" "	" "	"	19	7	35	Farnworth C.
Thompson Peter	Council Houses "	None	16	7	37	Wade Deacon Gra School
" "	" "	Holy Family	15	7	32	attending Farnworth C.t
" "	" "	"	20	7	34	Farnworth C.E
Critchley Louis	Smithy Lane "	"	20	10	30	Returned to Holy Fam.
Prescott Ernest	Liverpool Rd "	"	15	7	32	attending Farnworth C.
" "	" "	"	22	12	32	Left the Distr
Whitfield Samuel	Delpside	None	17	7	36	Farnworth C. attending
Prescott John	Liverpool Rd "	Holy Family	17	8	31	Farnworth C.
Pitt Eli	Townend Cronton	Farnworth C.E	20	7	34	Farnworth C.E
Pitt Edward	Cross House "	None	20	8	30	Under Age attending
Berry Fred	Chapel Lane Cronton	Farnworth C.E	15	7	32	Farnworth C
Collison Frank	Town End Cronton	"	17	7	36	Widnes Centre School
Lyons John	Roundabouts "	"	19	7	35	Farnworth C.
Lyons John	Roundabouts "	None	19	7	35	Farnworth C.
Elkington Albert	Fox's Bank Farm "	Farnworth C.E.	15	8	32	Gone to Farnw
Reynolds John	Elsinore Cronton	"	20	7	34	"
Harding Dan Alfred	Chapel Lane "	None	19	7	35	"
Prescott Ernest	Liverpool Rd "	None	24	10	30	Left District
Dimon Harry	" "	None	24	4	31	Left Distri
Reynolds John	Elsinore Cronton	None	20	7	34	Farnworth C.E
Foley Robert	Chapel Lane Cronton	None	24	2	33	Left District
Harding Dan Alfred	Chapel Lane "	Farnworth C.E.	21	7	33	Ht Farnworth
Prescott Ernest	Liverpool Rd	Cronton C.E	17	11	30	Left Distr
Whitfield Thomas	Delpside Cronton	Simms Cross, Widnes	21	7	33	Left District
" "	" "	None	21	7	33	Left District
Stanley John	48 Gossage St	Simm's Cross Widnes	19	7	35	Wade Deacon's Grammar School
Whitworth Wm Arthur	56 Gossage St	" "	21	3	36	Widnes Burb'l Sch

NUMBER		DATE			NAME	BIRTH			Whether exemption from Religious Instruction is claimed
Admission	Re-admission	Day	Month	Year		Day	Month	Year	
37		20	1	31	Cook James	29	11	1924	
38		20	1	31	Whitfield Dorothy	13	9	1927	
39		21	1	31	Winstanley Harold	6	2	1927	
19		11	2	31	Pitt Edward Enoch	21	5	1927	
40		16	2	31	Thompson Frederick Walter	16	6	1927	
41		23	2	31	Locke Ena	18	2	1928	
42		23	2	31	Hunt George Albert	25	11	1921	
43		9	3	31	Edwards Lorna	7	6	1923	
44		9	3	31	Berry Frank	7	12	1921	
45		24	3	31	Dutton Alice	27	3	1922	
46		24	3	31	Dutton Etty	30	3	1920	
47	20.6.31	13	4	31	Barber James	13	4	1922	
5	17.8.31	29	6	31	Critchley Austin Leonard	14	11	1923	
13	17.8.31	29	6	31	Critchley Winifred May	22	10	1921	
5	12.8.31	17	8	31	Critchley Austin Leonard	14	11	1923	
13		17	8	31	Critchley Winifred May	22	10	1921	
28		9	9	31	Harrison Henry Gordon	3	1	1927	
48	15.8.32	19	10	31	Twambley Enid Mary	3	7	1927	
49		11	1	32	Glover Sheila	20	5	1928	
50		19	1	32	Oagers Kathleen	15	10	1929	
51		23	2	32	Reynolds Caroline	26	1	1928	
52		4	4	32	Baldwin Eric Sidney	23	5	1927	
53		6	6	32	Hillyer Rose	31	12	27	
48	19.10.31	15	8	32	Twambley Enid	3	7	27	
54	57	15	8	32	Jones Vera	14	5	28	
27	25.9.30	15	8	32	Prescott Joyce Cox	7	1	27	
55		22	8	32	Stott Helen	9	8	27	
56		22	8	32	Stott Henry	9	3	27	
36	20.1.31	19	9	32	Cornes Alan	9	1	28	
53	6.6.32	9	1	33	Hillyer Rose	31	12	27	
57	54	13	3	33	Jones Vera	14	5	28	
58		13	3	33	Sidlow Alan Richard	19	2	28	
59		3	4	33	Beesley Doreen	27	11	27	
60		24	4	33	Garner Muriel	19	1	28	
61		24	4	33	Smith Alice Mal	5	1	27	

PARENT OR GUARDIAN		FORMER SCHOOL	WITHDRAWAL			
Name	Address		Day	Month	Year	Cause
Cook George	Hillside Farm Cronton	None	15	7	38	Widnes Central School
Whitfield Thomas	Delphside	None	21	7	33	Left District
Winstanley John	48 Gossage St Widnes	None	4	7	38	Farnworth C.E H
Pitt Edward	Cross House, Cronton	Cronton C.E	11	2	38	Farnworth CE School
Thompson Peter	Council Houses "	None	15	7	38	Widnes Certificate School
Locke Albert Victor	Chapel Lane "	None	21	7	39	Farnworth CE H
Hunt Albert	Penny Lane "	None	11	7	37	Farnworth C.E. Sch
Edwards John	Pex Hill	Farnworth C.E.	20	7	34	Farnworth CE H
Berry Fred	Chapel Lane "	None	27	2	33	Left the District
Dutton Ralph	Town End Lane "	Warrington Rd Widnes	29	1	32	Left District
Dutton Ralph	" " "	Warrington Rd "	24	3	31	Left District
Barber James	46 Gossage St	Simms Cross	21	7	33	Farnworth CE H
Critchley Louis	Smithy Lane Cronton	Holy Family	1	7	31	Returned to R.C Schol
Critchley Louis	" " "	" "	1	7	31	
Britchley Louis	" " "	" "	20	7	33	Returned to R.C Sion Convt etc
			15	8	32	Farnworth C.E
Harrison Harry	Stocks Cottage Liverpool Rd	None	20	1	33	Left the District
Twambley Patrick Peter	Chapel Lane Cronton	"	21	3	32	Under Age
Glover William	Rock Cottage, Town End	"	21	7	39	Widnes Central Sch
Odgers Tom	Leigh House, Chapel Lane	Simms X School Widnes	17	7	36	Farnworth C.E H
Reynolds John	Elsinore Cronton	None	21	7	33	Farnworth C.E H
Baldwin Sidney	Upton Farm	None	15	7	38	Wade Deacon Grammar School
Hillyer John	39 Muspratt St	None	18	8	32	Under Age
Twambley Patrick Peter	Chapel Lane Cronton	Cronton C.E	15	7	38	Widnes Central School
Jones Harry	Chapel Lane "	None	16	8	32	Under age
Prescott Ernest	Liverpool Rd	West Bank C. Widnes	22	12	32	Left the District
Stott Wilfrid	Foxall Al707	None	15	3	35	Gone to Farnworth CE
" "	" "	"	15	3	35	
Cornes David	Chapel Lane Cronton	Cronton C.E	21	7	39	Widnes Central School
Hillyer John	39 Muspratt St	Cronton C.E	25	10	34	Left District
Jones Harry	Chapel Lane Cronton	Cronton C.E	21	7	39	Farnworth CE H
John Arthur	" "	None	26	9	39	Left the District
Beasley Harold	24 Chapel Lane	None	17	4	39	Left District
Comer Archibald George	Fairholme Cronton Lane	None	21	7	39	Wade Deacon H
Smith William	Lowerhouse Farm	None	21	7	39	Widnes Central H

Admission	Re-admission	Day	Month	Year	NAME	Day	Month	Year	Whether exemption from Religious Instruction is claimed
64		21	8	33	Littler Frank	29	5	28	
65		21	8	33	Dutton Eunice	14	1	29	
66	72 see other	11	9	33	Pilkington Eric	13	4	27	
67		17	10	33	Cornes Rita	7	10	29	
68		13	11	33	Jarvis Winifred Phyllis	31	3	29	
	63	8	1	34	Dennett Douglas	30	11	28	
69		19	2	34	Lewis Gerald	31	10	26	
70		12	3	34	Sumner Kenneth Pilkington	24	7	28	
71		9	4	34	Jameson Barbara Florence	11	9	30	
72		23	4	34	Cornes Dennis Charlton	15	11	28	
	65	23	4	34	Dutton Eunice	14	1	29	
73		28	5	34	Almond James	24	3	29	
74		30	5	34	Cornes Noel	13	5	31	
75		4	6	34	Smith Rachael	31	5	30	
76		18	6	34	Cook Nancy	14	6	29	
77		20	8	34	Doad Barbara	25	10	29	
78		27	8	34	Bradburn Alma	25	8	34	
79		10	9	34	Baldwin Vivien	18	1	30	
80		12	9	34	Brannan John	12	6	30	
81		17	9	34	Brannan Jean	13	12	24	
82		29	10	34	Whitfield Kenneth Joseph	7	11	30	
83		4	2	35	Burgess Derek John	17	10	30	
84		25	3	35	Almond Dorothy	26	3	31	
85		29	4	35	Findlow Doris June	17	6	29	
86		29	4	35	Allyr Dorothy	18	7	30	
87		17	6	35	Walmsley Kenneth	17	3	29	
	74	24	6	35	Cornes Noel	13	5	31	
88		24	6	35	Pitt Hilda	16	11	31	
	66	21	10	35	Pilkington Eric	13	4	27	
89		6	1	36	Smith Nora	16	8	31	
90		6	1	36	Smith Marion	16	8	31	
91		13	1	36	Morris Leslie	7	3	26	
92		13	3	36	Lewis Lawrence Keith	10	5	29	
	84	1	4	36	Almond Dorothy	26	3	31	
93		7	12	36	Hunt Edna	1		32	
	85	11	1	36	Findlow June	17	6	29	

Name	Address	FORMER SCHOOL	Day	Month	Year	Cause
Littler James	Glebe Farm, Lunts Heath, Widnes	None	15	7	38	Left the District
Dutton Fred	Chapel Lane Cronton	None	13	9	33	Under Age Sickn
Pilkington John	Fox's Bank Farm, Tarbock	Whiston Central	19	7	35	Farnworth C.E.
Cornes David	Chapel Lane Cronton	None	19	7	40	Widnes Central School
Jarvis Wm Henry	Cronton, Smithy Lane	None	27	3	35	Left District
Dennett David	Hillside Terrace Cronton	Cronton C.E	21	1	39	Wade Deacon Grammar Sch
Lewis Jacob	5. Brookfield Crescent	Sutton Manor School	15	7	38	Farnworth C.E II
Sumner Wm	Council Houses Tarbock	Sylvester School	21	7	39	Widnes Central S
Jameson Ernest	Mill Lane, Cronton	None	18	7	41	Widnes Central S
Cornes John	The Nook, Liverpool Rd Cronton	None	21	7	39	Wade Deacon Grammar sch II
Dutton Fred	Chapel Lane, Cronton	Cronton C.E.	19	7	40	Widnes Central S
Almond Richard	Cronton Farm Cronton nr Widnes	None	19	7	40	" "
Cornes John	The Nook, Liverpool Rd Cronton	None	4	6	34	Under Age
Smith Wm	Lowerhouse Farm Cronton nr Widnes	None	17	7	41	Widnes Central Sch
Cook George	Hillside Farm Cronton	None	19	7	40	Widnes Central S
Dodd Robert	2 Cross Hillock Lane Cronton	None	7	11	35	Left the District
Bradburn Leonard	4 Brookfield Crescent Cronton	None	19	7	40	Widnes Central S
Baldwin Vivian	105 Upton Lane	None	1	9	39	Private School
Brannan Thomas Ed	Brookfield, chapel Cronton	Simm's X sch. Widnes	11	6	37	Simm's X C. Ch
" "	"		24	8	36	Widnes Central S
Whitfield Samuel	Delphside Cronton	None	17	7	42	H+ Farnhull's
Burgess Derek	Bus Cliff Smithy Lane	None	17	6	38	Left the District
Almond Richard	Cronton Farm Cronton nr Widnes	None	9	10	35	Under age
C/o Mr Cornes	Chapel Lane Cronton	Crosby.	22	5	36	Left the District
Hillyer Frank	Chapel Lane "	None	18	7	41	Widnes Central
Walmsley Harold	Cronton Smithy Lane	Elmore C School Widnes	7	9	39	Left the District
Cornes John	The Nook pool Rd	Cronton C. E	17	7	42	Widnes Central School
Pitt Edward	Cross House Cronton	None	1	2	38	Left the district
Pilkington John	Fox's Bank Farm Tarbock	Farnworth C.E.	15	7	38	Farnworth C.E III
Smith George Edgar	Stockswell House Cronton	None	1	9	39	Attends Private Sch
			17	7	39	" " "
Morris Jack	Whinney Lane Cronton	Farnworth C E	16	7	37	Farnworth C. E
Lawrence Lewis	Delphside Cronton	St Mary's Newton	17	7	36	Left the District
Almond Richard	Cronton Farm, Cronton nr Widnes	Cronton C.E	2	5	42	Hough Green Sch III
Hunt Albert	Penny Lane Cronton	None	15	7	43	Widnes Central
C/o Mr Cornes	Chapel Lane Cronton	Canada	19	7	45	Widnes Central